Praise for
GirlDad

"In *GirlDad*, Jay and his daughter, Rae Anne, lift the lid on the father-daughter relationship to reveal the richness, depth, and challenges that lie within. It is an uplifting and important read for any father or daughter who wants to deepen their relationship."

—**Meg Meeker,** PhD, internationally known pediatrician and bestselling author of *Strong Fathers, Strong Daughters: Ten Secrets Every Father Should Know*

"As we've come to expect, Jay delivers welcome insight and common sense for fathers. But what makes this book shine is how his daughter, Rae Anne, follows up with her own real-world advice that delivers a mandate for men to come alongside their growing daughters with love, faith, and even courage."

—**Josh McDowell,** international speaker, apologist, and author of more than one hundred books including *More Than a Carpenter* and *Evidence That Demands a Verdict*

"I cheered when my dear friend Kobe Bryant popularized the term 'girl dad.' And I'm delighted to say that Jay Payleitner and his daughter Rae Anne have captured the same vision with a book that will help create a lasting and eternal bond between countless fathers and daughters."

—**Pat Williams,** NBA Hall of Famer and author of *Who Coached the Coaches?*

"*GirlDad* is the best book Jay Payleitner has ever written. And there's only one explanation for this upgrade: his daughter Rae Anne! She says things her dad can't. So if you're a dad who's ready to learn about your daughter from a straight-shooter who gives the inside scoop on dilemmas you've faced and questions you've had in raising her, Rae Anne will become your new favorite life coach."

—**Michelle Watson Canfield**, PhD, LPC, author of *Let's Talk: Conversation Starters for Dads and Daughters* and host of *The Dad Whisperer* podcast

"Jay Payleitner's book, *GirlDad*, written with his daughter, Rae Anne, is outstanding. Rae shares fresh truths to dads of daughters, which are spot-on. Her poignant and honest insights will inspire you as a dad or be a great gift to a dad of a daughter. I highly recommend you get this book!"

—**Ken Canfield**, PhD, founder of National Center for Fathering

"As dads, we know our daughter will always be our 'little girl,' but the reality is that we had better learn to mature in relationship with her as she matures. That takes commitment and intentionality. Jay and Rae Anne have provided great insight for that rewarding journey. The charge to dads is to read this book with your daughter and commit to building the healthy relationship every daughter wants with her dad."

—**Rick Wertz**, founder and president of Faithful Fathering

"Jay Payleitner's latest book, *GirlDad*, isn't just his latest book. He's gone and done something dangerous that few authors have been brave enough to attempt. Not only has he asked for an opinion, but he's asked his daughter's opinion on each subject he covers in this book. It is fresh, real, and at times raw, as his daughter Rae Anne kindly disagrees or 'tweaks' his advice, and it works amazingly well. If you're a dad with a daughter and have wanted a book to help you parent your daughter, this is the one."

—**Todd Wilson,** founder of Familyman Ministries and FamilyManWeb.com

"As always, Jay has invested time processing the many aspects of family life. This time, with his daughter, Rae Anne, by his side, he shares valuable tips to enhance our relationship as dads with our daughters."

—**Dan Seaborn,** president and founder of Winning At Home

"Girls are different from boys—it's just true! So being a 'girl dad' will be different from being a 'boy dad.' Thank the Lord that we have an experienced duo like Jay Payleitner and his sweet daughter, Rae, to share their learned insights so that we may follow their path and not have to learn every lesson the hard way! I am so grateful for *GirlDad*!"

—**Brian Doyle,** founder and president of Iron Sharpens Iron and father of three boys and two girls

"Jay may be a veteran author on relationships, but Rae Anne is the superhero of this book. Her extraordinary insight takes this inspired book to heights a father can't reach on his own. After fifty-two years, I've finally developed a deep and trusting relationship with my daughter, Amy. This book gives younger 'girl dads' a practical and heavenly head start on creating a lifelong, loving relationship with their daughter or daughters."

> —**C. Marsh Bull,** president of Men's Group Foundation and author of *Saving the Corporate Animal, One Soul at a Time*

"Practical, honest, and real, *GirlDad* is a gift to fathers raising girls. As a father of four daughters of my own, this book has encouraged and equipped me to be the dad my girls really need. Thank you Jay and Rae Anne for teaming up to support dads and serve daughters so well."

> —**Jon Bechtle,** executive pastor of Chapelstreet Church, Geneva, Illinois

"This captivating book is a Payleitner-Daddy-Daughter-Pay-Stub into the very heart of their home movie life together. The script they first co-wrote on each other's hearts in real life is now showcased for us on paper in this inspirational collection of homegrown clips. With winsome creativity, this Payleitner pair reminds us to actually do what we already intuitively know: If we dads don't intentionally connect with our daughters . . . someone else will."

> —**Emmett Cooper,** founder and president of HoneyWord.org and author of the *HoneyWord Bible*

"In a world that often devalues the father/daughter relationship, the Payleitner writing team shows us just why it's so important. Jay provides a practical roadmap on how to love and encourage daughters, no matter how old they are. And Rae Anne adds a unique perspective that's both revealing and immensely valuable. This book is a must-read for every father who wants to raise confident and godly daughters."

—**Scott W. Kirk,** award-winning actor, playwright, and author

"Never underestimate the power of a father in a girl's life. If a father calls his daughter gorgeous, she'll believe it and remember those words even when she's old and gray. Dads are under attack in our culture, which explains why so many things are going wrong. This practical and wise book will help dads find their footing again in the home and in the hearts of their daughters. You'll learn what to say, how to say it, when to tap out, and when to swoop in for the save. I especially love the reality checks in each chapter by Jay's daughter, Rae Anne."

—**Arlene Pellicane,** host of *The Happy Home* podcast and author of *Parents Rising*

GirlDad

Girl Dad

A Father-Daughter Duo Discuss Truths That Impact a Girl's Heart, Mind, and Spirit

Jay Payleitner
Rae Anne Payleitner

SALEM
BOOKS
an imprint of Regnery Publishing
Washington, D.C.

Salem Books™ is a trademark of Salem Communications Holding Corporation. Regnery® and its colophon are registered trademarks of Salem Communications Holding Corporation.
Cataloging-in-Publication data on file with the Library of Congress.

ISBN: 978-1-68451-347-5
eISBN: 978-1-68451-436-6

Published in the United States by
Salem Books
An Imprint of Regnery Publishing
A Division of Salem Media Group
Washington, D.C.
www.SalemBooks.com

Manufactured in the United States of America

10 9 8 7 6 5 4 3 2 1

Books are available in quantity for promotional or premium use. For information on discounts and terms, please visit our website: www.SalemBooks.com.

To Rita Anne,

extraordinary wife and mother,

whose love and influence is found

on every page of this book about

dads and daughters.

CONTENTS

What's a GirlDad?

There may be some controversy in the terms "Girl Dad," "girldad," or "#girldad."

For most guys who pick up this book, the concept has the potential to be uplifting. A source of personal pride. You've got a daughter you love, you truly enjoy time with her, and you're committed to helping her fulfill all her hopes and dreams.

It also may be a bit unsettling. The title comes with expectations, wonder, uncertainty, and a heavy dose of responsibility.

Plus, the emotionally charged term has been usurped to promote a variety of causes and movements—some of which go to extremes and miss the bigger point altogether. Being a girl dad is all about love, respect, commitment, and finding long-term joy in the relationship you have with your daughter or daughters.

For further clarification, allow me to quickly suggest what "girl dad" is not. Especially in the context of this book, the term is not a political statement. It's not a feminist rallying cry. It's not a back-lash against the male ego. And it's not a fundraising or profiteering strategy.

Simply put, whether it's presented as one word, two words, or a hashtag, the term is a statement of personal commitment and appreciation made by men with daughters.

Worth noting: Others have trademarked these terms for use on clothing, jewelry, games, and other merchandise, leading to an outpouring of lawsuits. This book stands on its own. If you want to wear a T-shirt proclaiming your Girl Dad identity, go for it.

A Nod to Kobe and Gianna

The idea of a dedicated father proudly identifying as a "girl dad" has been around for a while, but the hashtag went viral in the wake of the tragic helicopter crash that took the lives of Kobe Bryant, his daughter Gianna, and seven others in January 2020. Looking to make sense of the tragedy, the shocked nation found comfort in recognizing and honoring Bryant for the unmistakable dedication he had to Gianna, as well as her sisters Natalia, Bianka, and Capri.

Media coverage quickly picked up on the idea. The most visible story may have come from ESPN anchor Elle Duncan, who shared the story of her first and only meeting with Bryant a few years earlier. In a *SportsCenter* segment the day after the tragedy, Duncan related how upon meeting the retired Lakers player, he noticed her pregnant belly and asked what she was having. When she said she was having a girl, he gave her a high five and said, "Just be grateful that you've been given that gift, because girls are amazing." The eighteen-time NBA all-star went on to say, "I would have five more girls if I could. I'm a girl dad."[1]

Elle Duncan's moving tribute to Kobe Bryant vaulted his self-proclaimed title into common usage. Though it initially referred to sports-minded dads and daughters, the definition of "girl dad" has expanded to include any man committed to encouraging and supporting his daughter.

The widespread use of the term proves that men raising daughters have a gut-level awareness that they need to be intentional about connecting with their growing girls. What's more, girl dads are eager to tell the world how much they love their daughters.

Kobe, thank you for your legacy. Not just on the court, but as a girl dad and lasting role model for dads of daughters everywhere.

Make It Your Own

No matter what the age of your daughter, feel free to label yourself a girl dad. Newborns, school-age girls, and young women all need to feel cherished by their fathers. Their future depends on it.

Dad, I think you already know the value of calling yourself a girl dad; it's one of the reasons you picked up this book. Your heartfelt concern about your daughter's future gives me the opportunity to remind you of a couple overarching principles: (1) It's a long journey, you will always be her dad, and you should expect bumps along the way, and (2) We're talking about her future, not yours.

I have an inkling of what you might be envisioning for your daughter, but I could be way off. Before turning another page, let's agree on this simple truth. Two or three decades from now, your daughter could be a missionary loving on hurting children on the other side of the planet, an aerospace engineer earning three times your salary, a stay-at-home mom with seven kids, or blossoming in any

Fathers vs. Daughters

For her first decade of life or so—beginning in those toddler years—you and your lovely daughter seem mostly to be of one mind and heart. You start out a little unsure, but she looks up at you as if you could do no wrong. Your time together is always precious. Because you're busy, she looks forward to every interaction. You regularly—and literally—sweep her off her feet.

Dad, you know exactly how to engage her. She brings you a silly drawing and you properly "oooh" and "ahhh." You vocalize a pretend conversation with her stuffed animals. You give her flowers at dance recitals and take her on ice cream dates. Maybe you even coach her soccer team. With a bit of effort, it's not at all difficult for a dad and young daughter to connect.

I endorse those moments. Absolutely. Daddy-daughter dates and life-is-good moments are critical when it comes to bonding with your little girl.

But this book is about much more than that.

Sometimes your relationship becomes dad vs. daughter. You and your little girl are not on the same side. You wonder, *How could this be?* But you also think, *I knew this would happen.* If you have not experienced that feeling of conflict, be patient. You will.

Take heart. This book is not a field manual for war. While you may occasionally do battle with your daughter, you really shouldn't approach your relationship with an attitude of "you vs. her." Mostly because you'll end up on the losing side. And so will she.

Instead, think of these chapters as a peace accord that will help the two of you do a better job of coexisting in a healthy truce. (The concepts presented in these pages work even if your daughter never opens this book. More on that in a moment.)

The term "girl dad" suggests that you and your daughter are *on the same side.* You have the same goals. You want her to grow in wisdom and strength, uncover her gifts, see herself as beautiful, do great things, and love deeply.

As her father, you want to develop a relationship of trust and honor so that you can be a welcome part of her life for decades to come. After all, she is going to need your input along the way. Which means you both need to *recognize your differences.* You need to acknowledge there's a distinction between the way fathers and daughters see the world. That should not come as a surprise. You're from different generations and you have vastly different life experiences.

And, of course, different genders. Raising sons is hard enough, but at least men have an inkling of many of the emotions, notions, and objectives swirling around the head of a boy as he grows into manhood. But in many ways, your daughter is from an entirely different world.

There's no doubt that caring dads of daughters are desperate for answers. I know that empirically. Several years ago, I wrote two books: *52 Things Sons Need from Their Dads* and *52 Things Daughters Need from Their Dads*. Guess which book sold twice as many as the other?

This book for dads of daughters digs a little deeper and is intended to make you think a little harder. But I think you're ready for it. You're done battling. You want trustworthy advice you can apply this very day.

Fathering Advice with a Contentious Twist

All that to say, this book is not your typical fathering resource. For sure, I promise to deliver my own best insight and loads of empathy, goodwill, and experience. If I do say so, what I have to offer is well worth your investment of time and money. But this book doesn't stop there. This book goes beyond my personal limitations. Way beyond. That becomes clear as soon as you turn to the *bonus pages* added to every chapter.

You see, a funny thing happened on the way to the publisher. Wanting to avail myself of every possible resource, I asked my daughter, Rae Anne, to *briefly* review what I had written. She loves me. She's brilliant. She has opinions. And she's brutally honest.

It turns out, Rae Anne was not brief at all. She spent weeks reviewing what I had written. And she made it better. More accurate. More revealing. More valuable.

My sweet and wonderful Rae didn't change what I had written. (I wouldn't let her.) Instead, she added page after page of indispensable honest and insightful commentary—sometimes turning what I had written upside down, but mostly, just making sure some critical points were not overlooked. In the book, we're calling those moments of counterpoint "Rae Anne's Reality Checks," and you can find at least one of those eye-opening sections at the tail end of every chapter.

What's more, she used her experience as a friend, small group leader, team captain, and visionary to add another dimension to the book. Based on real-life situations, Rae Anne came up with questions that fathers might be or should be asking, and she follows up with candid advice about your daughter that I couldn't begin to deliver. Look for that surprising Q&A under the subtitle, **"Hey, Rae Anne . . ."**

My daughter's intuition and insights that complete each chapter are the reason you don't have to insist your own daughter read this book with you. She can, of course. But our research shows that Rae Anne is pretty much sharing the stuff your daughter would be saying. I think you'll find my daughter's words to be a valuable gift.

Finally, of her own volition, Rae wrote some observations she is calling, "About My Dad." I let her say what she wanted to say. That was our deal. You'll appreciate her honesty and get some insider info on me—and gain intel on your own fathering successes and failures—that otherwise might not have been put into print. I guess that's only fair, I've been writing about Rae Anne and her brothers for almost two decades.

Maybe It Is a War

Talking with other dads and contemplating my relationship with Rae Anne, I have come to this conclusion: Fathers and daughters are, indeed, fighting a battle. But not with each other. We are in conflict with a wide range of forces eager to divide us and build walls between us. I can't let that happen. And neither can you, Dad.

It may help to think of the two of you—with all your differences—as wartime *allies* fighting common enemies. Weapons used against us include cultural expectations, past mistakes, traditions held too tightly, busyness, and blunders of miscommunication because of changing language, protocols, and technology. You may want to chalk up those divisive factors to the inopportune way life unfolds. But it's also possible that Satan himself is wielding those weapons of relational destruction. Either way, Dad, you need to be wary and ready.

Worth noting. Those differences which seem to be dividing you may actually be your greatest weapon. Dad, you have more than just your own wit and wisdom with which to fight back. Your maturing daughter also has been gathering her own arsenal of experience, instincts, and spiritual gifts. Combining forces—yours and hers—may be the greatest benefit of this book.

Really, It's All about Love

Figuring out who your daughter is and what she needs from you may seem like an intellectual exercise. And it is. You need to be a detective, looking beyond the obvious, uncovering her dreams and fears, identifying her friends and enemies, loosening her self-imposed shackles, strengthening her grip on what really matters, and being her greatest cheerleader.

But it's also an emotional commitment. As a committed girl dad, don't be afraid to open your heart and spill your guts. Not loudly. Never in anger. But saying, "I love you so much" is exactly what she needs to hear often and know with certainty down to her toes.

Meet Rae Anne

Hi, Dads. I'm Rae Anne, representing the first half of the title of the book in your hands.

Having read all of my father's previous thirty-plus books and having lived life as his daughter for the last twenty-eight years, I can tell you that inviting me into his pages is not something he does lightly. He has often asked for my input or opinion, but the words were always his. So when he asked me to be a part of this little adventure, I was curious why. And through the writing process, I think I finally figured it out.

You know how they say there are two sides to every story? Well, this book is the first of his to deliver on that promise—to speak to both sides. I am lucky enough to be the conduit for the viewpoint of the "girl" in "girl dad."

This is most assuredly my father's book, but in the last few pages of each chapter, I will be giving you a different perspective. Not just mine, as Jay's daughter, but the experience of my childhood friends who grew up in families different than my own; my high school classmates, who struggled with challenges different than mine; my collegiate and international friends, who I watched figure out who they wanted to be in their early twenties; and my adult colleagues and companions, who share with me the story of how they became who they are, and the dream of who they might yet become. Just as my dad looks to speak to each one of you and your experiences, I am looking to represent all the daughters I can.

I am my father's daughter in a lot of ways. We share a love for '60s television shows, commitment to regular debates around the kitchen table, and full appreciation for a well-crafted brain teaser and a well-turned 6-4-3 double play. But fair warning, we approached this book very differently.

My dad will give you insights and tools you are looking for and I hope to give you the perspective you need to effectively use them. There may be times when I will say something you don't want to hear or open your eyes to a subject you've never thought about, but I promise, you will be a better dad for it.

Trust me when I say I have not figured everything out. I have taken a few different routes in my life, I've had my fair share of successes and my own catalog of pain and disappointment. I cannot claim to be an expert on parenting, but I can rightfully claim my status as an expert on *being a daughter*, and that is what I will share with you in these pages.

CHAPTER ONE

Your Daughter's Hopes and Dreams

Every great dream begins with a dreamer. Always
remember, you have within you the strength, the
patience, and the passion to reach for the stars to
change the world.

—*Harriet Tubman*

Every little girl is different. Every season of life is different. And every woman is different. A father's job is to be a rock-solid foundation from which his daughter can move toward an uncertain future.

So prepare yourself. When it comes to hopes and dreams, you need to have pretty much the same response when your daughter says she wants to be an Olympic champion, a fashion model, the president of the United States, a drill sergeant, a hairdresser, a circus clown, an astronaut, or a mom. That response needs to be something like, "That's awesome. You would be great at that. Let me know how I can help."

Be sincere when you speak those words. Then back up that conviction by establishing an environment and providing resources which allow your little girl to dream big dreams, experience new experiences, explore her gifts, dare greatly, fail occasionally, face disappointment, and bounce back with a fresh supply of new hopes and dreams.

Can you do that, Dad? Feel free to partner with your daughter's mom in the role of cuddly nurturer in the here and now. But realize that fathers are typically charged with casting visions and shaping a child's worldview for the future. Then, helping children imagine their place in that world. The earlier you begin this process with your little girl, the better.

Insight for GirlDads: Join the Teddy Bear Picnic

One nice summer day, if you happen to look out your backyard window and see your young daughter serving lunch to a gaggle of non-human party guests, you already know what to do. Join the picnic. Dad, you have a standing invitation. Even though you are a mere mortal, you are more than welcome at any event your daughter hosts when she is small. Keep in mind, it may not always be that way.

I totally recommend you surrender to the fantasy and frivolity. Sit criss-cross applesauce on the blanket or tuck your knees up under your chin at the tiny table. Engage in spirited conversation with the other guests that may include stuffed bunnies and doggies, a Raggedy Ann, and an American Girl doll. Nibble on biscuits. Sip your "tea" daintily. Extend your pinky finger.

Little girls often create a make-believe world where all is well and wonderful things happen. It's a perfectly charming and appropriate way to spend an afternoon. For your daughter, the act of pretending opens the door to creativity, ingenuity, resourcefulness, and even future careers and life endeavors. By sharing that experience, you are proactively fostering her hopes and dreams.

Of course, it may not be a teddy bear picnic in your backyard. As your schedule allows, I encourage you to join your daughter anytime you see her assembling Lego starships, baking mudpies, hopscotching, chalk doodling, identifying cloud shapes, designing fairy gardens, dancing in the kitchen, or making up show tunes.

By the way, if your schedule does not allow you occasionally to join in your daughter's world, that may be a clue your schedule needs to be reprioritized.

Insight for GirlDads: Equalize Expectations

Whether you know it or not, your daughter is dealing with high expectations coming from two completely different directions. As she gets older, she may also have an unseen battle waging within.

On the one hand, she may be leaning toward a life dream that includes a modest education, finding the perfect hard-working and handsome man, and—for the most part—staying home and raising wonderful kids. Not a bad choice. But there is no guarantee of a fairytale ending. Several factors that may be out of her control must fall into place. But, if your daughter has painted that picture without undue influence by you or anyone else, then go ahead and help her lean into that dream.

Then there are all the voices from the other side. A generation of cultural movements has imposed bright young women—like your daughter—with a long list of expectations that can be both empowering and crushing. The declarations are emphatic: Get your degree. Get an advanced degree. Get a great job. Climb the corporate ladder. Break the glass ceiling. Don't get married too soon. Don't have kids too soon. Don't get married at all. Don't have kids at all. If your teenage daughter is leaning toward that kind of

ambitious career path, my advice is the same. Go ahead and help
her lean into that dream.

In other words, follow her lead. If she casts one vision, do what
you can to encourage her. But see if you can help her move forward
without closing the door on the flip side. If and when she changes
her mind, don't be surprised and don't judge. She may head off to
college in search of a husband and unexpectedly discover a field of
study that calls her name and is worthy of her full attention for an
extended season of her life. She also may find herself on track to
join the ranks of movers and shakers in some calling that will bring
her fame and fortune, when suddenly she experiences a profound
truth that shifts her focus and leads to less honor for herself and
more honor for God and others.

It's most likely that your daughter falls somewhere in the
middle. Career and family. Finding her place at home, at work, with
friends and family. Wouldn't it be wonderful if she found that elusive harmony and life balance that escapes so many of us?

A final word of caution regarding the push and pull of expectations: Your daughter will hear voices that chant, "Do something
worthwhile with your life." That's great advice. The problem is that
the individuals doing the chanting may have an agenda of their own,
which means they don't have your daughter's best interest at heart.

Insight for GirlDads: Think MBA. Think Politics. Think NCAA Scholarship. Think STEM.

Women have more opportunities than ever when it comes to
advanced education, collegiate and professional sports, corporate
board rooms, politics, and even the recent national emphasis on
science, technology, engineering, and mathematics (STEM).

Women make up about 56 percent of enrollments at U.S. colleges.[1] Women today earn more than 53 percent of all doctoral degrees.[2] More than six times as many women participate in college sports now than before Title IX.[3] The number of women in Congress has doubled in the last twenty years.[4] Over a recent four-year period, the number of women serving on corporate boards increased by 44 percent.[5] Finally, recent federal programs in STEM fields have established aggressive goals of recruiting women.

So why not your daughter? Shouldn't she jump on this bandwagon of aggressively pursuing fame and fortune on today's grueling career battlefields? Well, maybe.

Never suggest she can't do something because she's a girl. But also make sure that she doesn't turn her back on traditional female roles because she's bright, strong, and ambitious. Expose her to the vast array of choices she can make in today's world. Make sense?

Insight for GirlDads: The One Thing

In many ways, it doesn't matter what your daughter does with her life, except for one thing: She needs to do her best to find what God wants her to do. That's where she'll find contentment. That's how she'll do great things. That's how she can best give glory back to God.

Is there a secret to your daughter uncovering God's personal plan designed just for her? Go ahead and tell her—right out loud—to pay little attention to what the culture calls "success." That's an incredibly freeing concept for your growing daughter to understand and take to heart. Instead, with a sense of awe and humility, see if you can convey the idea that true fulfillment comes from pursuing the mind of Christ. If that sounds daunting, let her know that it's not about following blindly or robotically.

God has given her passions and longings. He wants her to follow her heart, explore new paths, and identify strengths, while heeding the moral compass of Scripture. Romans 12:2 says it well: "Do not conform to the pattern of this world, but be transformed by the renewing of your mind. Then you will be able to test and approve what God's will is—his good, pleasing and perfect will."

Insight for GirlDads: No Slacking Off

One of the great secrets to identifying God's call is for your daughter to roll up her sleeves, dig in, and give 110 percent to whatever project, puzzle, or assignment is right in front of her. That's the best way to identify her true gifts. Otherwise, how can she know if she should stay on one path or try another? The Bible offers this mandate: "Whatever your hand finds to do, do it with all your might" (Ecclesiastes 9:10).

Let's say your daughter has the chore of setting the table for dinner. She can toss the silverware every which way, set out glasses that don't match, and forget the napkins. When the family sits down, the disarray of the table is going to have a direct and negative impact on the dinner hour. Does she know that? Does she care? With a light touch, a father can let his daughter know there is honor in any and all tasks.

How about a couple of examples your daughter might find more relevant than arranging forks and knives? Let's say she likes dogs and expresses a desire to be a veterinarian. With your encouragement, she gets a minimum-wage job at the local doggy daycare. That's actually a great idea. But if she doesn't take the job seriously—keeping accurate track of food and meds and scrubbing cages with determination—she's really lost her opportunity to determine if working with animals 24/7 is right for her.

Let's say she's a whiz at computer science and expresses a desire to attend a prestigious engineering school. Because she's gifted, she may easily ace all her high school math classes, but she may not realize that thousands of other gifted students around the country are going above and beyond the routine classwork. Your daughter is not going to be happy when that rejection letter comes in the mail from her dream school.

To be fair, your daughter cannot give 110 percent to *everything* she does. But she *should* go above and beyond in some of those key areas that can shape her future.

Insight for GirlDads: Encourage, Don't Disparage

It's really okay if your young daughter quits soccer to spend more time on dance. In an effort to show your support, you may find yourself saying something like, "Good choice. I was getting a little tired of standing on the sidelines in the rain, anyway." Well, you know what happens then: A year later, she renews her interest in that sport you claimed to hate, and she throws it in your face every time you attend a game. Especially if there's a slight drizzle.

As we said, encourage the exploration of new endeavors. But don't be the one to close any doors. Better to say something positive and optimistic about her more recent choice. "Good choice. Make sure I know the dates of your recitals and competitions."

Insight for GirlDads: Teach Her That Seasons Change

Save this insight for her later teenage years. When she's younger, she won't be able to see the big picture. But your own life experience confirms that sometimes dreams or even entire areas of giftedness need to be set aside for a season for any number of reasons.

As your daughter begins to find her niche and gain positive reinforcement from peers, family members, teachers, and professionals, she will experience an occasional moment of truth. If it's a victory, celebrate. If it's an apparent setback—a potential dashed dream—you'll want to come alongside her and with a gentle spirit let her know that you understand her disappointment and acknowledge that you hurt for her. "I'm sorry, sweetheart. I know how important this was to you."

Later, after the initial grief and heartbreak have subsided, let her know that somehow, it's all going to work out. Never minimize her loss, but help her identify a slightly revised future. There will be other opportunities. Some right around the corner. Point out the hidden victories. There are almost always lessons in defeat. This may be a difficult season, but seasons change. Feel free to quote Ecclesiastes 3:1: "There is a time for everything, and a season for every activity under the heavens." Through it all, promise that you will always be there. Be that encourager she needs so desperately.

I know, Dad, lots of this sounds like a cliché. But more than anyone else, dads can get away with quoting scripture and using old platitudes. Don't abuse that privilege. Make sure sincerity and love comes through. She may shake her head and say, "Dad, please stop." But your words of hope and faith will resonate in her heart and soul. Really.

Insight for GirlDads: Your Daughter Can Be Anything She Wants to Be

That's one of those phrases straight out of the girl dad handbook. And I recommend it. Start when she's little and watch her eyes light up as her imagination takes over. More than any time in history, your little girl truly does have unlimited opportunity.

Go ahead and try saying it out loud: "You can be anything you want to be."

Please note, you're not saying she can be anything *you* want her to be. Or anything some boyfriend, high school counselor, well-meaning teacher, or magazine article wants her to be. The phrase is meant to empower her, not put her in a specific box.

Yes, you should have all kinds of discussions—at the dinner table, driving to competitions, tucking in at night—about all the fabulous options there are for a girl who works hard and makes wise decisions. There's a sense she will always be seeking your approval. But don't forget the eight words are "You can be anything *you* want to be."

There's another phrase paralleling that one you may also want to consider, especially in her teenage years. It's a little tongue-in-cheek, and her response may be an eye roll. But it makes a slightly different point. In the moment, it's congratulatory. But it also underscores the importance of looking toward the future. "I'm eager to see how you use all those gifts and talents over the next few decades. Promise me you'll use your power for good, not for evil."

You have so much influence, Dad. You may be tempted to steer her one way or another. But listen: I beg you not to burden your little girl with any of your own demanding paternal expectations . . . except one. As established earlier in this chapter, go ahead and insist that she seek and trust the guidance of the Holy Spirit. That's the one absolute Source of hopes and dreams that really matters.

Early and often pray these words over your daughter: "May the God of hope fill you with all joy and peace as you trust in him, so that you may overflow with hope by the power of the Holy Spirit" (Romans 15:13).

Insight for GirlDads: Find the Sweet Spot

To summarize this chapter: Dad, help your daughter identify her own giftedness and choose her own path. Walking that path with excellence and integrity is her best chance at living a life of true contentment. That's how she'll uncover and employ her unique abilities that lead to doing stuff that matters. Perhaps even great things.

Again, to be clear, this isn't about pursuing the culture's definition of success—like delaying marriage in order to climb the corporate ladder. The distractions and extremes of the world have a way of messing with a young person's mind. She needs to know that in many pursuits, there is a right and wrong. There are paths that lead to destruction.

What then is the secret to your daughter uncovering her best personal plan? Try introducing her to the idea of living in her sweet spot. Not living a life of excess, but also not settling for a life of deprivation.

Remind her of the secret found in Philippians 4:12–13: "I have learned the secret of being content in any and every situation, whether well fed or hungry, whether living in plenty or in want. I can do all this through him who gives me strength."

You don't want your daughter to think happiness is found in accumulating more stuff at the expense of personal relationships and peace, or exhausting herself with too many obligations and deadlines. But you also don't want her to see herself as unworthy or inadequate, hiding from the world and never exploring the opportunities she has to follow her dreams.

Dad, you can help your daughter find balance. Model for her the value of working hard and earning your daily bread, and trusting it's enough. Owning some nice things while properly taking care of them. Being good to yourself, but stopping to help a less fortunate soul along the way.

Too many young women today are careening down the road of life, bouncing off guardrails, completely off balance. They are afraid to take a stand and speak their dreams. Or they loudly insist they are the boss of the applesauce.

Your daughter has been blessed with gifts, passions, unexplored dreams, and a range of life experiences even at an early age. Help her identify her dreams and walk toward them with confidence and determination, with no hesitation. But not so fast that she loses sight of God's promised provision and the simple joys in life.

Rae Anne's Reality Check

Your daughter can't be anything she wants to be. My apologies to my father, but the nature of these Reality Checks is to bring his larger-than-life concepts back down to earth.

Your daughter will have talents and skills, and will certainly be given opportunities to succeed in any number of pursuits. With your help and encouragement, with some detours and probably a little pain, she will hopefully find fulfillment in her life's purpose and joy in what she does.

But she can't do *anything*. Of course she can't, just as you couldn't have done *anything* when you started on your life journey.

If your daughter struggles through freshman biology, she probably won't be accepting the Nobel Prize in Medicine. If she has played basketball for five years and still can't dribble with both hands, she probably won't be accepting a spot on a WNBA team.

The point is not that your daughter can do everything, because she can't. The point is that your daughter's *potential* could be anything. Even things you've never even considered. Don't place your daughter into a box of your own design. Don't limit her by your own experiences or view of the world. Truthfully, you have no idea what she is destined for or of what she is capable. Empower her to pursue greatness, to write her own definitions, and to seek her calling, whatever that could be.

Hey, Rae Anne . . .

My daughter doesn't know what she wants to do with her life. She is in college and doesn't seem to have any aspirations. Do I push her to pursue something, or do I leave her alone?

There are two questions I would have you ask yourself first. Does she truly not have any goals, or has she just not told you? The answer to this question can only come from an honest, nonjudgmental, nondismissive conversation about what she wants from life. Let her do the talking. Maybe she hasn't shared with you what she wants because she is afraid of how you will react. Maybe it's something you wouldn't expect or something she is still sorting out for herself. The important thing is to remember that whatever she is thinking about, whether you will approve or not, you want to be a part of the conversation. Your daughter likely is at a crossroads, and those are exhilarating and terrifying places to be. Let her know that she is not there alone and that you want to help her succeed.

Don't laugh at what she says, don't dismiss what she wants. Listen first, and wait for her to ask for your opinion. If you listen long enough, she will.

The second question would be: Is it a crisis of confidence or laziness that drives this lack of ambition? It is quite common for any young adult about to graduate college to be overwhelmed by the concept of the working world, where rental agreements and insurance payments loom. If your daughter hasn't quite committed to a specific discipline or career choice at this point, the threat of the adult world is becoming ever more ominous as she feels forced to make a decision that will alter the rest of her life. If this is the case, calmly reassure her that everything will be okay. Discuss her talents and skills and allow her to imagine the kind of career or calling she might enjoy. Also, talk through the types of things she absolutely *doesn't* want to do. Help her understand that it's okay if she doesn't know what she wants right now, as long as every day she takes a tiny step toward figuring it out. Maybe you can help her make those first few steps. Share tales from your own attempts at navigating career paths, job searches, job losses, and so on. Always remember that she is not you.

If the drive is not lack of confidence, but pure laziness, that's a different story. If you have worked through the above conversations and possibilities together and found that she is simply content to do nothing or feels entitled to a life she hasn't yet earned, a reality check of your own may be necessary. Remind her that while you do love her, you will only help support her after college if she is still working toward a goal or has a job of some sort. Maybe she needs to be thrown out in the real world in order to understand the necessity of hard work. Don't be afraid to take a hard line, and make sure your daughter's mother is on board if she is in the picture. But first, make sure you have these conversations with an open mind.

Hey, Rae Anne . . .
My middle school–aged daughter is constantly worried and distressed about her future. I see how hard she works, and I see her wonderful potential, but she only sees dark horizons ahead. How can I help?

Middle school is a dark place. Maybe you remember what it was like to be thirteen and awkward and thrown into a giant group with other awkward kids who are riding a hormone roller coaster. Maybe you've repressed it, but that is where your daughter is right now.

Every single middle school student is comparing themselves to the people sitting next to them, and most of the time, they feel inferior (see the aforementioned roller coaster). The popular girls feel stupid compared to the brainiacs, the brainiacs feel clumsy compared to the athletes, and the athletes feel ugly compared to the popular girls. It may sound clichéd, but the truth is every kid feels some version of this. It's a rite of passage of sorts. Not to mention that things have changed since you stumbled through your own middle school hallways. The world and all its opinions and judgment is much more present for your daughter—just a few keystrokes or push notifications away.

Your job through this trying period of the early teenage years is to shower your daughter with love. Your daughter is peering into the big void and may not know where to step next, much less see a clear path into a bright future. In some cases, a girl's hopes and dreams will help deliver her from the chaos of middle school. In many cases, she will look at the threatening void and hide in the maelstrom of makeup, cliques, and drama to avoid thinking about what lies ahead. Let your daughter know that she will make it through, that you love her, and that there is a good and life-giving path somewhere ahead of her that God has prepared, if she can just keep running the race (2 Timothy 4:7).

Have fun conversations about her dreams—even if they change every month. Help her get excited about high school, and gently remind her how working hard academically, athletically, socially, and spiritually will help equip her for success. Help her see that the future is exciting, the present is bearable, and your love is eternal.

About My Dad

To be honest with you, I have no idea what expectations Jay and Rita had on March 12, 1993, when they held their fifth child and only daughter in their arms. I imagine there was a bit of panic as they had no experience in raising girls—just four sons waiting at home for news of the birth. I also imagine there was a bit of nervous excitement for what this meant for the future of their family.

I imagine Jay had visions of someday walking his new daughter down the aisle and that Rita had visions of a partner against the boys she had battled for years.

Since that day, I have made a nasty habit of seeking hopes, dreams, and expectations for myself that I'm sure my parents never would have chosen for me. And it hasn't been easy for them. After four sons, I am the one who chose to join the Army and attend West Point. While the other four live anywhere from three hours to three minutes away from my parents' house, I am the one who chose to move across an ocean to Ireland. Between you and me, I don't see these strange choices or pursuits ending anytime soon, but don't tell Jay.

There have been fervent discussions, disagreements, and a few arguments throughout the years, but at the end of the day, I know my dad just wants me to be safe and loves me. The purpose of this segment is to tell you one thing: your daughter will surprise you, too. And don't you kind of want her to?

So, as hard as it might be, don't write her future before she has had a chance to start. When you are holding your daughter in your arms on the day she is born, laughing at your three-year-old playing princess, or nervously watching your sixteen-year-old on the debate team, *your hopes and dreams* for her should be the same: That she would love and be loved, that she will pursue what will give her joy, that she will find God's path for her, and that she will be protected, healthy, and safe. That's it. That should be your hope, dream, and prayer.

"If people knew how hard I worked to achieve my mastery, it wouldn't seem so wonderful after all."

—Michelangelo

CHAPTER TWO

Your Daughter's Teams and Teammates

*My dad drilled it in my head, you know, "If you want
it bad enough, and you're willing to make the sacrifices,
you can do it. But first you have to believe in yourself."*

—Jennie Finch, Olympic gold medalist,
2004 U.S. Softball Team

For many dads, sports are a natural connection point with their daughters. It's an arena in which guys often feel comfortable, and perhaps even knowledgeable. It gives us a chance to confidently share wisdom and experiences in the context of activity. One clear advantage is that a dad can spend time with his daughter in a gymnasium or on a field, and not every moment has to be filled with words. For many men, that's a relief.

I was never close to being a world-class athlete, but still I have loved every moment I spent coaching my kids, especially when they were between eight and twelve years old. At that age, they're just beginning to understand the beauty of sports. You're not just babysitting; the kids are eager for actual instruction. Most importantly, you still know more than they do. In a few years, they will think they know more than you.

Your initial instinct may be to coach only sports at which you excelled back in the day. But don't limit yourself. Personally, I mostly stuck to sports I knew and cared about—wrestling, baseball, and softball. But plenty of dads have had successful seasons coaching their daughter in sports they never played themselves. All you need to do is stay one step ahead of the girls on your team. Of course, the most important skills and disciplines you will teach apply to all sports . . . and life. That includes teamwork, sportsmanship, exploring new skills, diligence, and making the most of your potential.

My four years coaching young Rae Anne in softball, and later supporting her traveling softball career, may have brought us closer than anything else we experienced together. (Without those connecting points, this book certainly never would have been written.) We shared victories, losses, celebrations, and frustrations. We spent a lot of time driving across the state, waiting out rain delays, and checking into mid-range motels. At chain restaurants, sometimes we shared a booth, and sometimes she ate with teammates while parents and coaches talked about the challenges of raising precocious daughters.

I got to see Rae at her best and not-at-her-best. I saw her make friends, polish skills, and develop her gifts as a leader and negotiator. She saw me laugh, teach, organize, prioritize, and get kicked out of two separate softball games. And she saw me apologize for my poor sportsmanship on those occasions as well.

The forthcoming Insights will help you and your daughter make the most of her sporting life, whether that athletic career ends in early grade school or takes her through NCAA tournaments or even life as a professional athlete.

Insight for GirlDads: Your Daughter Does Not Have to Play Sports

Let me take that back. If at all possible, your little girl should spend at least a couple seasons on a local park district soccer team. Or maybe tumbling. Or some low-expectation physical activity that just about every kid in town experiences for a summer.

Like so many opportunities that will come along, she needs to "try" sports. She needs to test her skills and abilities. She needs to test her competitive drive and killer instinct. (Which she may not have, and that's okay.) Your daughter needs to have at least a couple pages in her scrapbook filled with team photos and participation ribbons to prove she once was part of a group of small children who had no clue what it means to be a sweeper, point guard, or shortstop.

Have her try some sports that are totally out of your area of expertise. You may never have participated in ice skating, dance, gymnastics, golf, or swimming, but one of those sports may be in her athletic sweet spot. You never know.

If she balks or exhibits zero talent, then back off. Your daughter can still have a long and satisfying life without ever scoring a goal or doing a backflip. The local high school varsity teams will do just fine without her, and you have the privilege of supporting your daughter as she explores a wide range of other options when it comes to hobbies, artistic pursuits, and other extracurricular activities.

The truth is that with most athletic endeavors, the time commitment is close to overwhelming. If and when your daughter gets serious about a sport, it may require twenty hours per week or more. Imagine what she could do if she devoted that kind of time to songwriting, poetry, sculpting, magic, ballet, debate, theatre, illustration, web design, robotics, pastry making, oil painting, stand-up comedy, biblical studies, and so on.

Plus, many of those non-sport activities still present opportunities to compete, lead, travel, and experience teamwork. So—if you read between the lines—much of this chapter still applies.

If she chooses not to be a "jock," you'll want to make sure she invests her newly reclaimed time in something other than texting, snapchatting, shopping, mani-pedis, chasing boys, and video games.[1]

Insight for GirlDads: Going to Games Is Just the Beginning

A dad who boasts, "I go to all my daughter's games" is missing the point. Showing up at game time is a no-brainer. That's commendable, but really it's the bare minimum. Actually, missing a game here or there because of other life commitments is not a problem at all. Your daughter will understand. An occasional absence may even help her better appreciate your faithful attendance!

One of the great benefits of your daughter's involvement in sports is that it gives you a chance to connect with her on a deeper level. For example, you may think driving her to practice is a chore. Instead, turn it into a chance to enter her world and give her a glimpse into yours. You may hesitate to give her athletic advice because you never played *her* sport. But turn that idea around! She knows things you don't, which means you can treat her like an expert and ask questions. That will lead her to engage you in new ways you never thought possible.

If you believe you can give her specific helpful instruction in an area, ask permission first. Sometimes she'll be receptive, sometimes she'll feel like working it out on her own. Again, asking open-ended questions and really listening goes a long way toward being a partner in her athletic success.

On those car rides to and from games and practices, keep in mind that silence is sometimes golden. You should be able to ask, "What are you working on?" and "How's the team look?" But steer clear of asking questions like, "Why aren't you getting more playing time?" or "Do you think you'll start the next game?" I hope you see the difference.

Insight for GirlDads: Make Sure She Has the Right Gear

Dad, you cannot jump onto the court or field in the middle of a game to adjust her stance. Also, there are no magic words you can use that will inspire her to greatness. But you can make sure she has the right tools to play her best at her current level. Some girls may be eager to spend their father's money. Others may hesitate, knowing you've already spent a tidy sum on team fees and other expenses. For you, Dad, investing—perhaps a little more than you think—in the right gear speaks volumes.

So ask if you can escort her to the specialty sporting goods store. Ask if there is some kind of training tool or even some special clinic or coaching she has been investigating. Not to add pressure, but to let her know you appreciate how hard she has been working. Sit with her to explore websites that offer relevant tools and instruction—not to throw away money on the most expensive equipment in the world, but to invest in skates, gloves, bats, sticks, helmets, cleats, and anything else that reminds her that you care and gives her a legitimate opportunity to take her game to the next level.

A slightly nicer tennis racket or softball bat might actually make a difference. But please wait until high school before investing a week's paycheck on a Dunlop Grand Slam racket or Miken Rain carbon fiber bat.

It's worth mentioning, Dad, that you should be careful your financial investment doesn't come with unreasonable expectations from you or lead to guilt from her if she comes up short. Even though you have sacrificed quite a bit of time and money in her athletic career, never throw that in her face. That's a rant you won't be able to take back.

Insight for GirlDads: It's Okay to Emphasize Winning

The first time you look at a gaggle of little girls with smiling faces, sequined sneakers, and fluorescent bows in their hair, you may feel a little silly talking to them about guts, determination, sweat, and digging deep to crush their opponent into mincemeat.

You may even be one of those dads who insists, "The most important thing is to have fun."

Well, that phrase drives me a little crazy. Now, I am a fun guy. Ask anyone. But I submit, *fun* is not a primary goal of most activities. More likely, it's a bonus byproduct. For example, baking and decorating confetti cupcakes can be fun. But the original purpose is to serve cupcakes. Playing Twister should be fun. But the goal is to tie your opponents into human knots so they fall over in a fit of giggles.

In the same way, softball should be fun. But the goal is to learn the fundamentals, practice well, improve your skills, and be competitive. Let me also take this opportunity to confirm that winning is the ultimate goal. That's why we keep score—and winning is fun.

Dads want our kids to be winners, and not just in preschool soccer. We want our kids to be winners in life. We want them to achieve positive outcomes in school, careers, and life. We want our kids to do more than just show up. We want them to set goals, practice, strategize, identify their strengths and weaknesses, over-come setbacks, partner with teammates, and experience the satis-faction of doing one's best. In other words, we want them to learn to compete with the goal of winning, right?

Insight for GirlDads: Some Things Are More Important Than Winning

If you are coaching your daughter's team, the following is an outline of a conversation you want to have with all the girls some-time in the preseason—maybe with their parents within earshot.

Establish the critical idea that winning is the goal of each and every game. Especially as teams get older, that means some girls will get less playing time. Some coaching decisions will be made that don't seem to make sense. Confirm that, early in any season, you will be exposing every player to a variety of positions and situations. Later in the season—especially in playoffs and key tournaments—you'll very likely double down on the goal of winning.

Once you get everyone on board—agreeing that "winning is important"—then you can open the discussion to the idea that there are, in fact, a few things more important than winning. Ask the girls to come up with their own ideas. You'll hear things like "hard work," "good sportsmanship," "trying our best," and "teamwork." You know what? All those things are more important than winning. You may even hear "family," "God," or "the pursuit of excellence." That's good stuff. But again, if someone says, "Having fun is more important than winning," feel free to stop and say, "I'm not sure about that. Sometimes we will be doing things that are difficult and not fun at all. But if we do the hard work . . . I promise . . . this season is going to be a blast."

Insight for GirlDads: Extreme Teammates

On the topic of winning and losing, each team on which your daughter plays likely will have girls who take it way too seriously and others who don't take it seriously at all. Dad, even if you wore dozens of jerseys in your prime, you may not have experienced this.

With boys' teams, the skill levels will vary, but the attitudes are mostly similar: each boy will practice with purpose, play to win, listen to the coach, see teammates as allies, and start thinking about the next game soon after any win or loss. In the dugout or on the sidelines, young male players may do silly stuff to keep it loose, but everyone knows the score. When the game is on the line, those motivated athletes understand it's time to dig deep and step up.

With girls' teams, some of the players on the bench will not even know who's winning. Girls who lean toward an easygoing extreme are much more concerned about the cute boy in the bleachers or how they look in their uniforms. Playing time is only important to them because their fathers routinely ask why they are not getting more of it. Those girls don't understand the idea of "putting on a game face," applying what's learned in practice, or hustling out to your position. Of course, that exasperates the girls at the other extreme who can't understand why their teammates are not as focused as they are.

These "extreme teammates" may even include your daughter. Your all-star daughter may be burning with a desire for personal excellence and see the other players—and even her coaches—as barriers to her success. Or she may be the opposite and really not care much about records, playing time, or scholarships.

Whether you're a coach or just a supportive dad, you need to be aware of the diverse attitudes of young female athletes—not so you can fix them, but so you can help your daughter anticipate the diverse attitudes among her teammates. Beyond just expecting this challenge, there are ways you can help your daughter be herself and see the bigger picture.

It may begin with determining why your daughter signed up for the team in the first place. If it's just for fun and exercise, that's all good. Cheer her on with zero expectations. If it's more a social thing, let her know that she really does need to honor the ambitions of her more serious teammates. Being on a team comes with responsibilities. That advice flip-flops for a daughter who aims high. She really shouldn't expect every teammate to compete at her level of focus and desire. But she also needs to figure out how to elevate the team when the situation calls for it. For example, early season practices can be a little loose, but those last practices before playoff games need to be focused.

Here's the bigger point. Wherever your daughter fits on the team, she needs to approach her teammates with the attitude that off the field, they all get along. If possible, she needs to learn to separate team dynamics and politics from the rest of life. She doesn't have to be best friends with everyone on the team, but there's a good chance a lifelong friend might *not* match her game-day attitude. Hopefully, you can imagine a state-ranked athlete getting along very well with a girl who is just playing for fun. Help your daughter envision that as well.

Insight for GirlDads: Expect Some Terrible Coaches

You may get lucky, but there's a good chance your daughter will have some terrible coaches—not including you—through her sports career. Honestly, on middle school or high school teams, she will pretty much have to learn to deal with it because those coaches are almost all teachers who have contracts, and removing them from coaching positions is a whole separate issue. Your job is to listen to your daughter's concerns. Don't minimize them. Encourage her to play hard, stay with it, and find ways she can succeed. You may think a level-headed, concerned father can go to the administration or athletic director to get a coach fired, but you can't. That's not how the system works. Your daughter will graduate, and that coach will remain. It stinks, but that's just the way it is.

With that basic understanding, you still have a responsibility to your daughter, her teammates, and your community. If there's suspicion of some kind of physical or sexual abuse, you may need to gather facts, take a stand, and make your voice heard. Even if she's in her mid-teens or older, your little girl needs to know her dad will protect her. Even if the situation doesn't change, she will have confirmation that you believe her and care.

While still intolerable, verbal or emotional harassment is more common and even more difficult to confront and challenge. Over the years, I may have missed the opportunity to fully support Rae Anne as she dealt with a couple of incompetent, mean-spirited, or even monstrous coaches. I did listen, but my advice typically was for her to rise above the situation and to channel her efforts into her role as an athlete and team leader. She survived those seasons, and may even have learned some truth about human nature and the world along the way—but as her father, I could have said and done more.

Your daughter will deal with people in authority—coaches, teachers, deans, bosses, neighbors, pastors, and so on—who will seem less than ideal. And there's a lot of gray area to move in. (In some cases, she may even be mistaken about them.) The best advice is probably to lean toward taking your daughter's side and building trust so that you can take advantage of teachable opportunities to help her see what's really happening. During those conflicts of life, your daughter will learn many valuable skills. That includes patience, empathy, humility, negotiation, discernment, courage, seeing the big picture, and turning the other cheek.

Insight for GirlDads: Rules Rule!

One of the great lessons of healthy competition is described in 2 Timothy 2:5: "Anyone who competes as an athlete does not receive the victor's crown except by competing according to the rules."

There may come a day when your daughter clears the pole vault bar that should have sealed the win at the track meet but is disqualified for wearing an illegal piece of jewelry—a multicolored string friendship bracelet. (True story.) Or her free throw doesn't count because she stepped on the line. (Happens every day.) Or perhaps more distressing, your college-bound shortstop is thrown out of a game for yelling at an umpire or kicked off the team for breaking an athletic code.

When these things happen, Dad, I encourage you not to storm onto the field, chase down the official in the parking lot, or hire a lawyer to get your child reinstated. In most cases, those responses will have negated any valuable life lesson and made matters worse.

Instead, let the natural consequences ensue. There are much more important things at stake than one game or one season.

Playing fields, courts, and stadiums are the absolute best place for your little girl to learn that rules exist. That includes both rules that are written and unwritten. Rules that seem arbitrary or unfair. Athletics may even open your daughter's eyes to the existence of rules set down by a loving God who knows everything about her and wants only the best for her. As she competes, look for teachable moments to reinforce the importance of rules. They're everywhere.[2]

Insight for GirlDads: Sharpen Her Skates

I don't know how to sharpen ice skates. But if your daughter is trying out for the hockey team or about to perform a figure skating routine at the local rink, that's a skill you'll want to acquire and apply.

You can't follow her out onto the ice. You can't force her to practice. If you didn't play hockey or figure skate, you really can't even give any final words of advice except maybe reciting one of the old standby lines: "Give it all you got." "Have fun out there." "Good luck, Zoe. You'll do great."

Please steer clear of final warnings clouded with negativity: "Don't let that new stick throw off your game." "I see that terrible judge from regionals is here." "Don't let your tendonitis distract you."

Tossing out a gentle positive vibe is a nice thing. No pressure, right? But you certainly don't want misgivings or hesitancy rolling around in her head as she laces her skates.

For dads of athletes or any competitors: maybe better than words are fathering actions. Weeks before the season, give her a chance to stretch her muscles. Take her to an open skate, to a batting cage, or just out in your own backyard. For those key tryouts or events, get her to the rink, field, gym, or auditorium a good half hour early. Have an extra bag packed with energy bars, water, and Gatorade. Sit in the stands, but not in the first three rows.

Invest in gear that helps bring out her best. Sharpen her skates, oil her mitt, install a ballet barre, erect a soccer goal in the backyard or a basketball net in the driveway. Do what you can and then let her go.

Insight for GirlDads: Your Daughter's Athletic Career Will End

Her first season playing softball for West Point, Rae Anne earned second team all-conference honors. It was a true privilege to follow her as the Army Black Knights took on Division I rivals like Utah, Georgia, and Villanova. Rita and I didn't miss many games, driving or flying to New York, Pennsylvania, Washington, Atlanta, and Orlando. When we couldn't be there in person, we watched streaming audio of the games featuring limited camera angles and amateur announcers. The overall experience couldn't have been more exciting. Because she was a Plebe (a.k.a. Army freshman), we were always unsure about how much playing time Rae would see. When she got in, she made the most of her plate appearances, finishing second on the team in home runs.

Her Yuk (sophomore) year was even more impressive. Rae Anne endured two concussions and torn ligaments in her left ankle, but she was still behind the plate playing catcher for a majority of games. The Army Black Knights swept the championship round, earning first place in the conference. Rae's first-inning, three-run home run highlighted the game that clinched the Patriot League championship and a bid to the 2013 NCAA tournament. I was there. (Rita was home awaiting the birth of our first grandson.)

The following week, Rita and I flew to Austin, Texas for the NCAA tournament. Army was eliminated after two games, but Rae Anne was flawless behind the plate, got a solid single and an RBI, and gave us memories we will cherish forever. Flying home, we were already eagerly looking forward to the 2014 season.

At the time, we didn't know we had just seen her last fast-pitch softball game ever. Long story short, her aggregate injuries had left Rae Anne unable to meet the rigid physical requirements required to continue as a West Point cadet. Her phone call stunned Rita and me. After thousands of innings, her softball career was suddenly over. Looking back—for a brief period—I was mourning my own loss more than Rae's. Not cool, Jay.

The takeaway for all fathers is this: Even if your little girl is the best in the world in some sport or other endeavor, don't put her in that box. See her as more than one-dimensional. Love all of her. When her career ends—at any age or stage—make sure she knows you are dedicated to every aspect of who she is and who she will become. Be cool.

That summer, in addition to recuperating physically, our multi-talented daughter stunned us again by announcing she would be finishing her college career in Ireland at University College Dublin. What's more, UCD doesn't even have a softball team.

Rae Anne's Reality Check

As your daughter's dad, you will and *should* want her to be an active member of clubs, sports, and a whole slew of activities.

However, there is a tendency for dads to go one of two directions in respect to sports for their daughter. The first (and the one that dominated the majority of Western civilization until the late '70s) is to steer their daughter away from sports and to more historically feminine pursuits. The second, and in many ways the opposite, is for fathers to jump at that chance for their daughters to follow in their own athletic footsteps in an attempt to find common ground.

I do firmly believe that if you are choosing between these two options, the second is certainly preferable. But both of the above directions are about *you*, when they should be about *her*. Don't get me wrong, I believe that every small child should participate in some kind of team-based, athletic, competitive pursuit. It teaches them about their own bodies, abilities, how to work with others and connect with adults other than their parents or teachers, and promotes physical activity in a fun way. These should be the goals when they are young. It does not matter if they are good.

But once she moves into an age of more self-actualization and development, I encourage you to focus on *making your daughter's hobbies your hobbies* and not the other way around. Follow her lead. It doesn't matter if she's amazing, and you see flashes of state titles and Olympic medals in her future. If her dream doesn't match yours for her, don't catch yourself steering her into a sport or hobby of your choosing. That's when living vicariously through your children gets dangerous.

There is a definitive difference between helping your daughter overcome fears and challenges in competition and finishing commitments and forcing her down a path of your own making. Trust me on this. I have seen it play out dozens of times: girls will continue to play sports for years beyond their own desires because it's what their dad wants, or it's the only time they see their dad. That just leads to resentment and a lot of wasted hours that she could have spent finding her own path.

Don't try to overrule your fifteen-year-old freshman when she says she wants to do musical theatre over basketball. No matter how beautiful her three-point shot is or that D1 scholarship looks down the line, you have to trust that she knows what is best for her, and that you've equipped her to succeed in anything she puts her mind to.

Rae Anne's Reality Check

If you choose the treacherous and exhausting path of coaching your daughter's team (something I highly recommend, for the record), I would like to warn you of a few things up front.

First, expect to get caught up in the winning and losing, the parent drama, the playing-time struggles, all of it. That's inevitable. Whether you're coaching eight-year-olds or sixteen-year-olds, all of that will happen.

Second, you may want to pay attention to when you should stop coaching. To quote my dad from the beginning of this chapter when he was encouraging you to coach kids between the ages of eight and twelve, "Most importantly, you still know more than they do. In a few years, they will think they know more than you." I would like to take that one step further and say that if they stay in their sport long enough, especially if it's a female sport that you never played, there will come a day when they *do* know more than you. I am not saying that means you should stop coaching them, but maybe that's the day you can find them a coach to take them to the next level. Make sure you are coaching for them and not for you.

But most importantly, in the midst of coaching your daughter and her teammates, you need to find the balance of Father vs. Coach. Not an easy task. I learned the perils of this both as the daughter of a coach and as a player on a team where the coach was someone else's dad. It doesn't matter if your daughter is the best player on the team or the worst. For the good of player development at the younger levels and the responsibility of putting a winning team together at the older levels, you may have to start your daughter, sit your daughter, pull your daughter, or even rebuke your daughter. That's what coaches do.

She may not be your best player, but she needs to know, at all times, that she is your favorite player. This may seem obvious or even ridiculous to you. Of course she's your favorite. But when you have to start someone else above her, or get a pinch hitter for her because it's the right move, she has to know that she is still your favorite girl on the team. You can achieve that by talking with her honestly about the decisions you make as a coach and proving to her off the field that you love her as a father.

Rae Anne's Reality Check

I want to take a moment to talk about fun. This elusive concept seems to be the center of every conversation in the history of youth sports. A lot of phrases come to mind: "Winning is fun," "As long as you are having fun," "Having fun is the most important thing," etc. We throw this word around a lot, but never really discuss it.

Allow me to illustrate with a story from my very first coaching experience. I was home for the summer from college, and a former coach of mine asked if I could join the coaching staff of a ten-and-under softball team that was falling apart mid-season. Now, I never pictured myself coaching ten-year-olds; high schoolers were more my sweet spot. But I wanted to help out my old coach, so I jumped in.

It became very clear within the first few practices that the team was divided right down the middle. The head coach (and father of the team's main pitcher) believed that because these girls were now part of a club/travel team that played in tournaments and required lots of off-season training, and in-season practices as well as traveling, that winning should take the priority, and the best girls should play most of the time. The other faction of the team was driven by an assistant coach (and father of a pretty decent infielder) who believed that because these girls were mostly eight and nine years old and in their first season away from the local recreational league, that every girl should play every position and learn. He believed there should be a rotation, nonchalance, and the focus should not be on winning, but on "fun."

And then there was me. I walked into this cesspool of animosity as soon as I stepped foot on the field. Truth be told, both of these men were right and wrong. They were living in the extremes (and I do believe genuinely had good intentions), when the answer lay right in the middle. No one was having fun on this team, and the wins weren't happening either.

With these opposing sects in front me, an obvious tension in the air, and twelve girls who didn't know which way was up, I realized there was a decision to make. And it wasn't "fun" vs. "winning"—it was what was I going to do for the next 120 minutes of practice. So I did what I knew how to do. I set up some drills, taught some skills, answered questions, and talked to the girls about the game. They learned about the importance of getting lead runners out, and I told some stories about my experience between the lines. I was only with them for six weeks, and I didn't solve all their problems. What I did do was try to share with them my love of the game.

It is easy to say that you need to do both: Have fun and figure out how to win. But the practicality of that is much more of a tightrope than you would expect. My takeaway from twelve or so years of competitive athletics and almost thirty years of life is that there are practices, days, and stretches of time that are exactly zero fun. And sometimes you don't win.

I think it's dangerous to claim fun as the main goal of anything in life. Claiming winning as the goal is troublesome, too. Because while fun is wonderful, necessary, and uplifting, and winning is a rush, powerful, and satisfying, what you really want is *joy*. Joy is richer and longer lasting, and more valuable than just about anything in this world. Joy comes from loving something. When you love something, you work hard at it, you fight for it, sometimes you get frustrated with it, it challenges you, and sometimes it's exactly zero fun. Sometimes you don't win. But it's worth it.

My takeaway from those six weeks was pretty simple. Yes, let the five-year-olds throw water balloons one practice, let your twelve-year-olds finish early for an ice cream-eating contest, let your varsity team play their dads in a bragging-rights match—but never miss a chance to teach, inspire growth, or to share your joy and help those kids find their own. I promise a few wins and some fun along the way. (It's clear I'm not just talking about coaching, right?)

And let me tell you, there was a moment in the last tournament of that summer when I watched in amazement as our infield turned a double play, and that was the most fun I saw them have. Not because we won (I honestly don't remember), and not because of some superficial attempt at fun, but because they got better in that moment—and they enjoyed it.

Hey, Rae Anne . . .

My teenage daughter hates her coach. I'm not sure of the details, but I know they don't get along and that she comes back from practice fuming. I don't know if I can or should help.

Like most career athletes, I have had a multitude and variety of coaches throughout the years. Some I got along with, and some I didn't. Having been raised in a family with four athletic brothers, I quickly came to understand and respect sports, winning, and competition from an early age. So when a coach yelled, disciplined, or had high expectations, I was not easily offended. Some girls, especially in adolescence, get wrapped up in the drama. That all being said, there is a line you should look for. It is typically a good thing for your daughter to be challenged, and it builds her character to have to listen to and respect a coach with whom she doesn't get along. But if you see your daughter being hurt, then it's your job to step in. While this applies to your daughter's physical well-being (e.g., being forced to play while injured or skipping water breaks as a punishment), at the moment, I am more concerned with her emotional well-being.

I had a coach who genuinely made me begin to hate the game of softball that I loved so much because he continually tore me down. Over the course of a year, his hate infected my joy. Now, I was seventeen. I did not want my father to intercede or pull me off the team, but he stepped in in another way. He listened to what I had to say and built me back up when I was torn down, and the next year helped me find a team with a coach who helped restore my love of the game.

You will always want to protect your daughter. That will never change. But know there will be battles you can fight for her and battles you can only hope you have equipped her to fight through on her own.

About My Dad

In two or three of my father's other books, including *52 Things Kids Need from a Dad,* he confesses to having been a "Jerk in the Stands." My father was a very "passionate" man about all his kids' athletic endeavors. This enthusiasm would often manifest itself in pacing along sidelines and yelling from bleachers.

Now, I have to give him credit for two things. One, he never yelled at his kids or any other athletes on the field, reserving his unwelcome input for umpires, referees, and coaches for the opposing team. Two, he has gotten much better.

According to my oldest brother, Alec, I never truly saw the worst of it. When I played my last season, Jay managed to deal with his frustrations in the West Point bleachers quietly. For that, I am grateful. My point here is that fourteen-year-old Rae Anne often understood and agreed with the things he was shouting; *most of the time, he was right.* But that didn't change the embarrassment of having to squat behind the plate in the catcher's position and have the umpire with whom I had been friendly the whole game say to me, "That guy needs to relax."

Most dads are going to embarrass their daughters at some point along the way. But I suggest you let it be for things like gym shoes that are too white or an inability to understand cultural references, not for flying off the handle over a referee's call in front of their teammates and coaches.

"It's supposed to be hard. If it wasn't hard, everyone would do it. The hard is what makes it great."

    —Tom Hanks as Jimmy Dugan, *A League of Their Own*

"I am building a fire, and every day I train, I add more fuel. At just the right moment, I light the match."

    —Mia Hamm, *Olympic gold medalist, 2004 U.S. Women's Soccer Team*

CHAPTER THREE

Your Daughter's Friends

*Friends are those rare people who ask how we are and
then wait to hear the answer.*

—*Ed Cunningham*

One of the great joys of writing this book is that I know if I get
something totally wrong, Rae Anne is going to correct me. In
several instances, you will find her chapter-ending insights much
more valuable than my paternal musings. When it comes to the topic
of girls and their friends, I am going to lean hard on my coauthor for
clarification and applicable wisdom.

Here's what I do know. Your daughter will have somewhere
between five and five hundred friends in her life, and her dad should
never attempt to categorize them or suggest that some are more or
less worthy of her time. A dad just doesn't know what any single
friend or group of friends provides for her during different seasons
of her life. At different times, friends can give your daughter a sense
of belonging, strength to overcome disappointment, courage to act,
acceptance when she feels abandoned, wise counsel when she has

a decision to make, and freedom to be herself when the world is telling her to be someone else. Those worthwhile benefits barely scratch the surface.

On the topic of friendship, other truisms should also be kept in mind. Sometimes opposites attract. Sometimes birds of a feather flock together. Sometimes two heads are better than one. Sometimes three's a charm. Sometimes there's strength in numbers. Dad, when you meet a new friend of your daughter, keep in mind that first impressions count, but don't judge a book by its cover.

The Bible confirms the value of even having one good friend in Ecclesiastes 4:9–10, "Two are better than one, because they have a good return for their labor: If either of them falls down, one can help the other up. But pity anyone who falls and has no one to help them up." So Dad, if your daughter has a legit friend, that's a three-part win right there. Her work will be more effective. She'll have support during any rough patch. And her heart will be open to helping others in need.

Insight for GirlDads: Where She Finds Friends

For the most part, dads really can't do much to help their daughter *make* friends. But you can create an environment where she can *find* potential friends and also give her space to nurture those relationships.

When she's young, it may begin—quite literally—by your choice to live in a neighborhood with sidewalks where the houses aren't too far apart. That may seem like an oversimplification, but I am convinced interactive and close-knit neighborhoods have generated more childhood friendships than all the prearranged play dates ever scheduled by well-meaning parents. When a young girl rides a Big Wheel down the block or creates a hopscotch court on her driveway with colored chalk, it's a magnet for future friends to wander outside and join the fun.

Of course, the same spirit of community can happen in a kid-friendly apartment building, family housing on a military base, a rural setting with lots of cooperation between farm families, or any living environment where young people get a chance—or are even obliged—to interact with other kids. Growing up with suburban middle-class sidewalks in front of our house helped all of my children make long-lasting friends. That may not be your situation or style, but you get the idea.

That same formula works as they get older. Put your daughter in proximity of other kids, doing something fun, with zero parental pressure, and watch like-minded kids gravitate toward each other. If she's up in her room clicking on screens, she may never make any true friends. Fake digital friends come and go. Real-life interaction, such as the crucible of sports or mounting a theatre production, creates an environment in which participants begin to count on each other. That interdependence leads to emotions and feelings of trust, sacrifice, encouragement, and empowerment—all the elements of a true friend.

Beyond the classroom, school offers a wide range of extracurricular activities from yearbook staff to canoe club. With your gentle encouragement, your daughter's gifts, talents, and curiosity might lead to all kinds of activities that involve other kids and naturally offer a bit of freedom and downtime required to build friendships. That might be community theater, dance troupes, after-school enrichment activities, library and park district programs, summer camp, youth groups, 4-H clubs, Girls Scouts, American Heritage

Girls, School of Rock, even tech-centric clubs that involve gaming, anime, programming, robotics, video, and graphic design.

It's worth remembering: Dad, you can't instruct your daughter to be friends with any one particular child. But you can give her opportunities to cross paths with potential friends. Lifelong friendships often begin simply because two people happen to exist in close proximity. That includes sandbox friends, next-door neighbors, schoolbus seatmates, creative colleagues, high school lab partners, and college roommates. Still, you never know. The best example of that is two toddlers whose moms happen to be best friends. Those two little ones will inevitably be forced to share each other's company. Whether they immediately like each other, grow to like each other, or never really get along is not for Mom or Dad to decide.

Insight for GirlDads: Advice You Can Give

As stated, your daughter will choose and make her own friends. Still, there are a few pieces of wisdom you can pass along. Don't blurt these insights out all at once. Also, you'll want to deliver them with a tone that says *this might work*, rather than *here's how*. Most of this advice won't come as a surprise.

To get a friend, be a friend. This wisdom parallels the well-known verse, "Do to others as you would have them do to you." (Luke 6:31)

Be yourself. If your daughter changes who she is to lure a friend, she's going to end up with a friend who doesn't know who she really is. That would force her to keep pretending until the inevitable not-so-friendly blowup.

Don't gossip. Sharing quality dirt she's heard about some kid in school may seem like a way to become part of an exclusive inner circle. But actually, it puts up red flags. Friends will inevitably share secrets. But gossiping proves to potential friends that your daughter can't keep secrets!

Make small gestures. The loudmouth or show-off gets attention but won't make many authentic friends. Instead, encourage your daughter simply to be herself and be kind. To smile. Say, "Hi." Make eye contact. Offer a helping hand. Offer a genuine compliment. And tell her to make sure she herself is approachable. Dad, you can't instruct your daughter to walk up to someone and say, "Hey, wanna be friends?" But you can remind her that other girls—just like her—are also looking for friends.

Expect situational friends. Not every good and dear friend is going to be a forever friend. Let your daughter know it really is okay to have a friend for a season. When summer ends or the project is complete, fond friends sometimes go their separate ways and sweet tears may be shed. Plus, who knows? That short-term friend could come back in your life at a later date.

Share your own friend-making stories. This idea comes in handy, especially if your daughter expresses frustration with her lack of friends. You (and your daughter's mom) can surely look back and spin a few tales from your own uneasy history of finding friends. If your efforts were initially pathetic or unsuccessful, that's even better. Remember to end with a hopeful success story.

Insight for GirlDads: Encourage Diversity

This is a note for both you and your daughter. Just a couple generations ago, most teenagers made friends with other teenagers that came from a similar background, wore similar clothes, had similar hairstyles, went to the same house of worship, and had the same color skin.

Dad, when it comes to your daughter's friends, diversity is a good thing. She probably already knows that, but you initially might be surprised when she introduces her newest pal. Dad, you probably don't have to say anything except, "Nice to meet you."

Having friends from different backgrounds and beliefs will serve your daughter well as she moves out into the world furthering her education, seeking a vocation, and sharing her faith.

Heaven itself will be filled with men and women from every culture. Revelation 7:9–10 describes the scene:

> After this I looked, and there before me was a great multitude that no one could count, from every nation, tribe, people and language, standing before the throne and before the Lamb. They were wearing white robes and were holding palm branches in their hands. And they cried out in a loud voice: "Salvation belongs to our God, who sits on the throne, and to the Lamb."

Insight for GirlDads: BFFs Will Change

When it comes to the identity of your daughter's friends, make no assumptions. The neighbor girl who walks with her to the bus stop every morning may be a best friend or not a friend at all. Same with the girl who costarred with your daughter in the youth theatre musical. Same with the catcher who helped your daughter practice pitching. Same with the girl you noticed in the rearview mirror chatting with your daughter when you did your last carpool run.

Once your daughter verbally describes a companion as a "best friend," you still might want to wait a few weeks before using those words. The term has a sacred overtone. If you're overheard saying something like, "Jenna is going to a movie with her best friend," you might be corrected in no uncertain terms.

What's more, that girl who was clearly her best friend two weeks ago may not be any kind of friend at all today. In other words, don't be surprised if you get a death stare from your teenage daughter when you suggest, "Why don't you have Molly come over and help with that?" There's no way you could know it, but she and Molly may no longer be speaking.

Finally, I'm pretty sure the term "BFF" is out of vogue with teenagers. Using the acronym will likely get you a well-earned eye roll and an honored place in the parenting hall of shame.

Insight for GirlDads: Her Posse

Don't panic if your daughter becomes part of a tight-knit group of friends that puts out the vibe of being exclusive and even a bit self-important. In general, there's a significant benefit to being a valued link in a circle of friends. Not a clique that feeds on itself and pressures members into teasing or bullying those who are not in the group, but three, four, or five girls who share interests, build trust, accept each other's differences and preferences, cheer victories, and comfort each other through losses.

Your job, Dad, is to see if you can unobtrusively figure out what motivates these girls. Even if it seems to be constructive and positive, you'll still want to encourage your daughter to maintain her own identity. She shouldn't have to change to fit in. Make sure she sees value in herself beyond that circle of friends. Even though she may be busier than ever, she still needs one-on-one time with you, Dad. You're the best person in the world to help her realize her value as an individual beyond that group of friends.

Be warned: Any clique, street gang, or posse will give rise to a leader who establishes an agenda or attitude. That girl won't be difficult to identify. Her name and opinions will be esteemed as if she has cornered the market on all of life's great truths. If that leader is your daughter, then you have double responsibility to monitor the life and impact of this band of sisters.

It's worth noting: the idea of peer pressure often gets a bad rap as it leads young people down a dangerous path, but don't discount the value of positive peer pressure that can help your daughter or her friends steer clear of unfavorable decisions. It begins with kindness, compassion, respect, and self-respect learned in the home.

Insight for GirlDads: When She's Feeling Like an Outsider

Of course, there's a flip side to cliques, especially for anyone excluded from them. In middle school, just finding a place to sit at lunch can be a big deal. When your daughter isn't invited to a social event or included in some minor activity, a father may instinctively try to dismiss the severity of the snub. Telling your devastated daughter that "it's not the end of the world" is the exact wrong thing to say. Instead, listen. Empathize. Acknowledge that her feelings matter. Even be a little sad for her. Realize, you may not be able to "fix" this.

Timing is critical. You may have the perfect advice, or your immediate inclination might be to call the school or set up playdates for your daughter. But don't say or do too much too fast. Instead, first focus on validating her emotions, making your home a safe space, and reminding her that finding and keeping friends is a tricky business for every one of her peers.

If she's being bullied or rejected, be careful not to minimize her pain. Cuddle her up and affirm your unconditional love. Be ready and willing to consult an outside counselor to assess her for depression and thoughts of self-harm.

It's possible, Dad, you may not see the severity of this concern because of gender differences. *Forbes* magazine recently reported on a study showing the rate of self-harm among girls is more than triple the rate of boys.[1] To some degree, that's a very real possibility if your daughter is being ostracized or bullied.

What else can a dad (and mom) do to help when your daughter is feeling left out? Take a timeout from friendship frustrations and do something special as a family. Pray together for all your relationships. Be your daughter's advocate, but also help her see that she needs to develop her own voice and strategies when it comes to friends and peers.

In a longer conversation—after some of the initial hurt has passed—you will want to help your daughter think through why she is being left out. It's not easy, but some judicious self-examination may reveal that she gets a little bossy, whiny, selfish, critical, manipulative, or mean. Go easy here. You should be able to coach her in improving her social skills, but it's best if she comes up with these personal insights on her own. When in doubt, focus on your daughter's positive traits, rather than making her feel unworthy of friendships.

Finally, with an open mind and spirit of partnership, you may want to approach the parents of the girl who seems to be excluding your daughter. Don't make accusations. Admit there are two sides to the story. After all, both families want what's best for all the girls involved. What's more, your ultimate goal is to equip your daughter to be her own advocate and learn the delicate art of making friends.

Romans 12:16 may deliver the best advice on cliques, peer pressure, and fitting in,

> Live in harmony with one another. Do not be proud, but be willing to associate with people of low position. Do not be conceited.

Insight for GirlDads: Boys Who Happen to Be Friends

The above insights have been referring mostly to your daughter's friendships with other girls. But the truth is that your daughter may have an equal number of friends who are boys. Those relationships bring up an entirely fresh set of questions for dads.

Chapter Seven covers "Your Daughter's Boyfriends." Certainly, friends who happen to be male can morph into boyfriends at the speed of sparks. As a matter of fact, sincere friendship can be a healthy segue to lasting romance. You may have your own story to confirm that idea. Of course, you don't want to make any assumptions regarding your daughter's guy pals. Which means you need to figure out the right way to ask your daughter about the intentions of that young man who keeps hanging around or coming up in conversation. It might be as simple as asking, "Are you and Micah together or just friends?" Expressing some version of that straightforward question when Micah isn't around should be something you feel comfortable doing. Feel free to turn it into a dad joke: "So, you and Micah? Is he just a placeholder or is this the beginning of the romance of the century?" You may or may not get your answer. Joking when Micah is around would probably be a bad decision.

In some ways, you initially need to treat male friends the same as boyfriends. Curfews may be earlier. Bedroom doors remain open. Certainly no overnights. As your daughter gets older, being honest with each other is a proven way to build trust. If she says, "We're just friends," then you need to believe her.

Celebrate all your daughter's friends. Strong, healthy, committed relationships in her youth will lead to, well, a better chance at developing strong, healthy, committed adult relationships. Maybe think of it this way: For your daughter, your family is a boat-building dock and, as needed, a port during the storms of life or even an anchor. Good friends can be a sail that helps her catch fresh wind from any and every direction that may take her places you've never dreamed of.

Rae Anne's Reality Check

I am going to jump right in and address my dad's last insight: boys who happen to be friends.

It is one of my great beliefs that what we need in this world is more platonic love and more opposite-sex friendships. I think everybody wins. We have so much we can learn from each other. As much as I appreciate a good Billy-Crystal-and-Meg-Ryan flick, men and women, and boys and girls, not only can be friends, but arguably should be encouraged to be.

As my father indicated in his earlier insight concerning the importance and wonderful nature of diversity in friendship and how it can make everyone stronger, I encourage you to view opposite-sex friendship the same way.

Let me ask you, as the loving and protective father that you are: when romance does enter the equation for your daughter, do you want that to be the first time she is trying to forge a connection with a male peer? When she is chock full of romantic feelings and middle-school hormones, do you want that to be the first time she tries to really talk with a boy? Trust me, you want your daughter confident in her ability to interact with that guy she is interested in, comfortable speaking her mind around young men, laughing honestly, and treating herself as their peer. On the other side of that coin, don't you want those young potential suitors to see your daughter as a complete and valuable person before anything else?

This is the power of friendship. The more we teach this next generation to look at everyone as people first, the better off we are. If your daughter has built some true male friendships leading up to her romantic pursuits, she will be so much more successful in finding the right person. These friendships start when we are very young.

Instead of what you may have mostly accepted as cultural norms, I would like to challenge you here and invite you to think logically with me. While I do understand, as my father states above, the need to put safety rails in place as your daughter enters the preteen years, can we just agree to let children be children? Let's not call your daughter's male friend her "boyfriend" or make fun of her "future wedding" to him. Why have adults always been in such a rush to add the concept of romance to places where it doesn't yet belong? My guess is, kids don't think about these things until we make them aware of them. So let's let them be children, playing tag or Candyland or Fortnite.

In every phase of my life, I have had incredibly important male friends who helped shape who I am. Even today, I still count many male friends amongst my best. Married men, single men, handsome men, goofy men. And they all speak into my life in different ways. Now, I was lucky: with four older brothers and the ability to hold my own on grade school flag football fields, I was comfortable around boys from a very early age, unlike many of my peers. But I think that if we as adults can change the way we view these relationships, the people, the marriages, the friendships, and the men and women of this next generation will be better off for it.

Hey, Rae Anne . . .

I think my daughter might be one of those "mean girl" bullies. She's not the friend I thought she would be. What do I do?

The answer to this question is largely determined by how old your daughter is. Even the nicest of girls will go through a nasty phase at some point between the ages of eight and eighteen. So perhaps this is a fleeting issue that you can coach her on a few times, and she will work her way out of it.

However, if this appears to be more of a permanent aspect of her personality, or if she is on the older end of the spectrum, it is important to know that mean girls do not disappear at high school graduation: they continue to wreak havoc into adulthood.

The first step in attempting to address this concern is to look for a source. While a girl must own her own actions, there tend to be three sources of "mean girl" behavior: her parents, her friends, and her own insecurity.

Really look at yourself and your daughter's mother and see if you have reinforced this behavior through speaking negatively of other parents or having an air of superiority, whether justified or not. This is a difficult question to ask, but it may bring to light something you can work on as a family.

You can also look to the influences of her friends. You become like the people you spend the most time with. Your innocent daughter might be mimicking the actions of her meaner friends.

Then there is her own internal source. At the heart of almost every mean girl is insecurity, and to be fair, at the heart of almost every teenager is insecurity. This is just one example of how it manifests. Mean girls are desperate to mock so that they won't be mocked. Whether your daughter is a mean girl or just an average teenager, I can guarantee that you cannot express enough love to her. Even if she rolls her eyes, even if she seems embarrassed. You should be the voice in her head telling her that she is enough.

Whatever the source, when it is revealed, make a change. Condemn her behavior, help her uncover the source of her actions, make her apologize, encourage more positive friendships, make changes in yourself, and reinforce positive self-talk and candor. The lesson to impart to your daughter is that though there might be a *reason* for this behavior, that doesn't *excuse* the damage she is doing. This is not an easy thing for a parent to admit, and it's harder to fix. But this is an area in which a dad can make a difference. Be forthright and partner with your wife. Help your daughter be a supportive friend and grow into a loving woman.

"Do not be misled: 'Bad company corrupts good character.'"
—1 Corinthians 15:33

CHAPTER FOUR

Your Daughter's Mom

*A mother's arms are made of tenderness and children
sleep soundly in them.*

—*Victor Hugo*

A s a girl dad, you might think your greatest asset is your
charming personality, wisdom gained through experience,
hope for the future, and overflowing love. Well, you would be
wrong.

All those things are quite valuable. But for most fathers, your
greatest asset is the woman who gave birth to your little girl. Ideally,
that's your wife, with whom you share life, love, and frequent conversations. Sometimes it doesn't work out that way. Still, no matter
what, you will increase the chances of being the dad you want to
be by partnering with the woman you're thinking about right now,
whether she is your wife, your ex-wife, your ex-girlfriend, or your
daughter's mom, stepmom, favorite aunt, grandmother, and so on.

You get the point, right? You want your little girl to look up to
you. But you also want her to have a woman in her life with whom

she can talk about girl stuff. Hopefully, that adult female loves your daughter nearly as much as you do. This may be a challenge, but you also want someone who will hold you accountable when you need a gentle reminder or priority adjustment regarding your role as a dad. Wives especially are good at that, but only if you humble yourself and open the door to their wisdom.

The forthcoming insights remind you that your daughter's mom is an asset, not an enemy.

Insight for GirlDads: You Were Never a Girl

Dad, there are things women experience that you never have and never will. And I'm not just talking about giving birth and breastfeeding.

After a generation of trying to prove otherwise, researchers are finally admitting there are differences between boys and girls. Some of it is basic anatomy, some of it is brain chemistry, some of it is learned behavior, some of it is cultural expectations, and all of it adds up to the different ways girls and boys journey through life. Even at a young age.

You are well aware of many of these differences. For example, you have never experienced an obsessive desire to dye your hair. You have never asked another guy to accompany you to the bathroom. You never doodled hearts and flowers on your chemistry notes. You never changed clothes three times while your date was waiting downstairs. You never stressed over choosing a one- or two-piece bathing suit. You never bought a device to make your curly hair straight or your straight hair curly. You never threw out a pair of pants because they made your butt look big. You were never the only girl in a science club. You were never bullied or teased because your breasts were too big or too small. You never intention-ally gave the wrong answer in class because you didn't want to be labeled a brainiac. You never worried about your mascara running. You've never been dumped (or ignored) for no reason at all by a guy you thought was nice.

Plus, you typically brush off gossip and insults while your daughter takes hurtful words very, very personally.

Men, it's okay if you're not in the loop when it comes to all things female. In these areas of concern, your most important job is to make sure your daughter has a strong female role model with whom she can share her heart and heartbreaks. If you're lucky, that woman may then share a little bit of that information with you.

Insight for GirlDads: Be the Husband Your Wife Needs

If you are not married to your daughter's mother, this insight may bring you a wave of regret. My apologies. Still, read on. The information below may be useful to you down the line. Or you can pass it on to your future son-in-law.

If you are married to your daughter's mom or stepmom, then pay close attention. Building and modeling a healthy marriage is a priceless gift you can give your daughter. It makes her life—and yours—easier.

The following fourteen quick points are highlights from my book *52 Things Wives Need from Their Husbands*. Ready?

- Cherish your wife. Women need to feel loved and honored. Even if they are strong and independent, they need a man who would die for them.

- Don't say stuff you already know will tick her off. No one knows your wife like you do. You know her trigger points. Every time you walk in the door, you could start an argument. So don't always say what you're thinking.
- Don't keep score. Too many guys think they are making tremendous sacrifices for their brides. But if you're really honest, you would admit that she puts more effort into the marriage and family than you do.
- Really listen. When she wants to talk, put down your phone, turn off the radio, and turn your face in her direction. When you go out, don't eat dinner at sports bars. The game on the big screen behind your wife will be a constant distraction.
- Fall on the grenade. Expect to apologize more often than she does. Three reasons: (1) As risk-takers, we mess up more. (2) As men, we know how to take one for the team. And (3) Women are the gatekeepers when it comes to romance. When we finally do apologize, the real question is "What took us so long?"
- Nag-proof your life. Instead of flopping on the sofa when you walk in your front door, say, "Is there anything that needs doing around here?" If she says yes, then meet her needs with a smile. But most of the time, she'll say, "No, dear," and you'll be off the hook.
- Be the pastor in your home. Here's the formula: Do. Model. Teach. Here are some examples: Pray—let your family see you pray; encourage them to pray. Tell the truth—let your family hear you speak only truth;

encourage them to be truthful. Read the Bible—let
your family see you reading the Bible; encourage them
to read the Bible. Volunteer—let them see you volunteer; invite them to join you. Your wife wants and needs
you to lead your family spiritually. Do. Model. Teach.
- Cleave to your bride (see Genesis 2:24, Matthew 19:5,
and Ephesians 5:31). Choose to only have eyes for her.
Love her every wrinkle, every gray hair, every extra
pound. Flee pornography. Instead see only her. Her
smile. Her eyes. Her hidden beauty. Remove all competition. Your bride is the most beautiful woman in
the world.
- Rage not. Proverbs 14:29 says, "Whoever is patient has
great understanding, but one who is quick-tempered
displays folly."
- Get the job done in the bedroom. Talk about it.
Ask her what she wants. Be creative. But not too
creative.
- Stay married. Every time I speak, guys come up to me
who say they want to be great dads, but they live
across town or across the state from their kids. Instead
of thinking up reasons to divorce, spend that same
effort looking for reasons to stay married.
- Surprise her with gifts. Come on, dude. You know she
loves flowers, chocolate, and little gifts. It's so easy,
but we don't do it. And it doesn't have to be expensive.
It really is the thought that counts.
- Kiss your wife in the kitchen. This is the best—and
most fun way—to give your daughter a sense of

security. Seeing that romance exists and even escalates after the wedding day gives her a reason to postpone sex. Gentlemen, your daughter also is peeking at your kissing technique. So look your beautiful wife in the eyes, hold her face gently with your hands, tell her you love her, and then kiss gracefully for two, three, or four seconds. If your daughter says, "Hey, get a room," then you know you're doing it right.

- Anticipate the seasons of marriage. Your bride will make mistakes. You will disappoint her. Kids will exhaust both of you. Kids will exhilarate both of you. Friends will fail you. Jobs will be lost. Cash will be tight. Illness will come. Let all of life—the good and bad—bring the two of you closer together. Trust love.

Summarizing, I fear that a high percentage of young people these days are cynical about the idea of making a lifelong commitment to another person. Help your daughter see that traditional marriage is the building block of family, community, and our nation.

Insight for GirlDads: Your Ex Is Not Your Enemy

Some dads reading this are in a constant battle with their daughter's mother. Since the divorce, you've essentially agreed never to be in agreement. About anything. If you fit that description, you will not be surprised to hear that your bitterness, disregard, and animosity are doing damage to your daughter.

So stop it.

To be honest, I can hardly imagine what you're going through. I don't know what it's like to be separated or divorced, wondering what happened to my marriage, scraping up child support, and scrambling for any chance to see my daughter. If that's your current scenario, then my heart aches for you and every member of your family.

For the sake of all your kids, allow me to offer a three-part strategy for interacting with your daughter's mother. Plus, an assignment.

First, demonstrate common courtesy. Treat her at least as well as a neighbor, coworker, or stranger on the street. Be decent.

Second, respect her role as a mother. She may not exhibit all the classic and desirable maternal traits, but your daughter needs to see that you respect the very title of "mother." Refrain from shouting, blaming, or name-calling. Admit that she may have gifts and insights you lack.

Third, keep open the lines of communication. Fathers and mothers need to share information about the kids. That includes schedules, deadlines, victories, failures, friends, enemies, dreams, fears, and frustrations. Withholding information is divisive and counterproductive. Finally, don't use the kids as a messenger service.

The assignment, then, is this: Put yourself in your children's shoes. It doesn't matter how old they are; when parents are in conflict, their offspring suffer a range of painful emotions. Guilt. Fear. Confusion. Anger. Torn allegiances. Grief. Shame. Sadness. Loneliness. Anxiety. A little empathy goes a long way.[1]

Anything you can do to minimize this anguish is worth the effort. It may be delivering a long and sincere apology to your daughter for your responsibility in creating the situation. You don't have to drag out all your dirty laundry or disclose all your misdeeds, but modeling sincere remorse is hugely important. Working toward a lasting truce or peace accord with your ex will lead to a happier future for all.

Insight for GirlDads: Take Your Wife's Side

In the early years, the mother-daughter relationship boasts a wonderful innocence: "When I grow up, I want to be just like you, Mommy!" But as soon as a growing girl looks in the mirror and begins to see her mother, that all changes.

Around that same time, your daughter is going to come to you because "Mom's not being fair" or "Mom is just being stupid." And that kind of statement is followed up with "Dad, do something . . . talk to her!"

Suddenly you're caught in the middle. First, of course, you explain that your daughter has to respect her mother. Then, because you're a good dad, you listen to her very persuasive arguments about a later curfew, fewer chores, getting her own phone, getting her own credit card, skipping family gatherings, piercings, tattoos, why an R-rated movie is not really that bad, and why something that's not okay really is okay because everyone is doing it.

Then what do you do? Tell your daughter you will honor her request and "talk to Mom." Then, keeping your word, you talk to Mom. Then—in almost every circumstance—take your wife's side.

There's tremendous value in showing a united front. When it comes to matters of consequence, parents need to stick together and provide a reasonable and justifiable case for why their collective decades of experience and wisdom carry more weight than teenage immaturity and ignorance. (By the way, please don't use those two words with your daughter. That would just add fuel to the fire.)

Talking with Mom behind those closed doors, you shouldn't expect to immediately be on the same page on every concern. Some issues will be a bigger deal to one of you or the other. Engaging in healthy debate with your daughter's mom is actually the goal. Many of your parenting challenges require some lengthy discussions and strategy sessions. Remind your wife about teenage boys. Let her remind you about teenage girls. Share insights, fears, gut feelings, and warning signs.

In addition to putting your own two heads together, seek insight from a variety of sources. Go on fact-finding missions to glean knowledge from other parents, online parenting forums, biblically based resources, and youth pastors. Perhaps together, listen attentively to your daughter as she presents her case. But when the time comes, make sure you and Mom are on the same page. As coparents, you need to decide and firmly present what the two of you truly believe is the best for your daughter.

Insight for GirlDads: Surrender with a Smile When They Gang Up on You

Your sweet wife and your even sweeter daughter are destined to have a relationship quite different from any you have ever witnessed. During the second decade of a girl's life, she and her mother might be best friends and worst enemies. One minute, they may share a sweater, a scarf, earrings, or a necklace. The next day, one of them is expressing outrage at a snag in that sweater or lost piece of jewelry. Not to mention the clashes over territorial rights in the kitchen, powder room, closets, and even the refrigerator. Other touchy subjects (which dads should never mention) are makeup, hairstyles, weight loss, time spent in the bathroom, and menstrual cycles.

There are plenty of occasions the two most important women in your life will be in disagreement—which means you should be overjoyed when they are in agreement, even if that means they have joined forces to gang up on you. Dad, you're tough. You can take one for the team. Plus, you know deep down they love and admire you.

Over the years, when Rita and Rae Anne have chosen to mock my cargo shorts or white socks and sandals, it makes me glad. They are laughing together. When the two of them disregard my suggestions and we end up at a restaurant, movie, or destination of their choosing, that's also a good thing. When they simultaneously groan and roll their eyes at me because I use some out-of-date slang from the 1980s, I am secretly delighted. Sometimes I even do it on purpose.

Insight for GirlDads: Honor Their Choices

When a son says, "Dad, I want to be like you," that's pretty cool. But it's also cool when a son doesn't join the family business or chooses to exercise gifts and talents that his father never imagined. We've all heard stories of a farmer's son who becomes a world-renowned brain surgeon. Or a shopkeeper's son who makes it big in Hollywood.

In those situations, a father feels nothing but pride and admiration. However, it may be a little different with moms and daughters. A career-minded woman might feel a little betrayed when her daughter announces that she is not going to use her college degree and instead stays home to raise kids. On the other hand, a stay-at-home mom might feel spurned or envious if her daughter jumps right into a lucrative career in business or technology.

Smoothing out those feelings might not be that difficult. For you, Dad, the goal is to help your daughter and your wife see each other's perspective. You're talking about different eras and different experiences. Remind your wife that the two of you have always been committed to raising your daughter to be strong, independent, and make her own choices. Remind your daughter that her mother has spent much of her life making sacrifices for the family. Acknowledge that life decisions are difficult, and that her circumstances will evolve if and when a husband, kids, and unexpected opportunities come along. Celebrate and support each season of life.

This Insight is really another reminder that the role of women is changing. Indeed, the pendulum swings both ways. Communication and unconditional support will serve your family well.

Insight for GirlDads: Mom Doesn't Need to Know Everything

You shouldn't keep many secrets from your wife. But a few non-earth-shattering secrets between a father and his daughter can enhance your bond. (In some cases, you'll want to let your wife in on the secret without letting your daughter know. Hopefully, Mom doesn't feel snubbed and instead willingly goes along with the ruse.)

The secret could be a silly song, favorite fishing spot, or unspoken tradition known only by you and your daughter. Maybe it's how you stop for frozen yogurt after sporting events. It could be a charm for her bracelet that has a secret meaning. It could be paying cash for a pair of $120 jeans mom said were too expensive. It could be a secret wink, whispered word, or inside joke. A daddy-daughter secret, of course, is not meant to exclude Mom. It's meant to solidify the almost magical relationship between a dad and the little girl who will always be his little girl.

TOPICS FOR MOMS ONLY

Following is a short list of topics you don't want to talk about with your daughter. And neither does your daughter. Still, they might come up. If they do, answer any question with as few words as possible and eliminate all thought of dad jokes. Feel free to pass most of these concerns over to Mom.

Topics include puberty, menstruation, cramps, PMS, facial hair, body hair, acne, body odor, bras, underwear, feminine hygiene products, and gynecological exams.

In an emergency, single dads especially may have to be ready to field these kinds of concerns. All dads should expect to make an urgent run to the drugstore without asking any questions.

Rae Anne's Reality Check

I would like to make a comment on the sidebar about mom-only topics. Here's the thing: While my dad is right—these are most likely not topics you want to discuss, and most likely not topics your daughter wants to discuss with you—how you *respond* to situations that arise around these topics is incredibly impactful to your daughter.

Whether you can appreciate this or not, these topics will be some combination of exciting, terrifying, shameful, and foreign to your daughter, at any given time. While you can't ever fully understand, you are going to be two things for her while she navigates these waters: 1) The first man to be around her in these situations and 2) Her dad.

I am not asking you to bust out a slide projector or walk her through the mechanics of specific measures, but you will actually be crucial in her ability to accept herself and these changes she is going through. Don't let your discomfort over a subject get in the way of your daughter's ability to feel comfortable in her own home. This very prevalent stigma and shame that girls and women have felt about their own bodies largely begins when they feel like they have to hide tampons in their closet or whisper about their struggles so as to not "disgust" the men around them.

You get to be the first man in her life when these changes start, and your ability to speak on the subject without fingers in your ears and say words like "period," "tampons," and "vagina" out loud help reassure your daughter that everything is gonna be okay, there is no shame to be had, and that you love her in the midst of the chaos. If you need to practice saying those words, practice in the mirror. If you need to educate yourself so you can be the support system she needs, buy a book. Finally, if you can, teach your sons to do and be all these things alongside you. They'll need to be trained for marriage to someone else's daughter someday, too.

Hey, Rae Anne . . .

There is some kind of war going on in my house. I'm not sure how or why it started, but my wife and daughter are either arguing with each other or not speaking. I don't want to get into the middle of it, but I don't want to be collateral damage either.

I am going to guess your daughter is in her early teenage years, and the topic they are fighting over isn't really something that you are going to easily understand. Chances are, this dispute will subside soon enough and they will return to the love half of the love/hate relationship many teenage girls have with their mothers. The key is to keep talking to your wife, behind closed doors especially. She needs you to listen and help figure things out. Not necessarily to solve the conflict, but she needs to know you have her back and you will be her sounding board.

When it comes to your daughter, obviously continue to cultivate your relationship with her, but not at the price of badmouthing your wife or breaking her trust. Remember that while your daughter may beg for you to defend her or take her side, she is also watching how you behave as a husband to your wife. This is a valuable chance to model what devotion, respect, and a united front means in a marriage. That's an attitude she will want to cultivate in her own future relationships. So basically, don't get into the middle of the fight, but make sure that when the dust settles, both females know you stand behind your wife.

Your job is not to solve the dispute. The best way to get your lives back to the hormone-fueled normal that you know and love is to partner with your wife to equip your daughter to solve it herself.

Hey, Rae Anne . . .

My wife and I are going through a nasty divorce, and it is not something that can be fixed or resolved. I desperately don't want my daughter to get caught in the crossfire. What do I do?

Nasty divorces tend to come with nasty emotions. What you need to remember is that whatever happened between you and your wife, she is still your child's mother. Do not let your daughter hear you say horrible things about her mom, because that does two things: One, it tarnishes the view she has of her mother, which will surely affect their relationship and your daughter's development. Two, she will witness real hatred in you. You are probably dealing with a lot of emotions right now, but work through them with your lawyer, friend, therapist—someone, but not your daughter. You do not want to be the person who teaches her what hate, anger, and pain are; that is the world's job. You need to be the one laying the foundation for her to have love, forgiveness, and hope.

You should also realize that while your marriage may be ending, your ex-wife is most likely not going anywhere. For the rest of your life, she will be around—sharing custody, at parties, at weddings, with grandchildren—so you are going to have some kind of relationship with her even after the divorce. Do you want hate and anger to constantly infect, warp, and poison your lives and relationship each of you has with your daughter? Work now to build at least a semi-cordial, amicable relationship with your ex, for your daughter's sake. Watching friends, classmates, and teammates endure their parents' breakups, I've witnessed both extremes. I'm not sure there is such a thing as a good divorce, but you need to at least attempt to minimize the anguish. In a longer conversation, remind your daughter there was once a love story, as far away as that might seem to you now. There was even a happy ending to it—your daughter's birth.

With that in mind, the last point I would make is that your daughter is going to mourn the loss of her parents' marriage. She is going to mourn the loss of her family home and the love that unified all of you. Her heart will be broken. So do not dismiss her pain; allow her to mourn. And shower her with affection. Make sure she never questions her father's love. With the dissolution of your marriage, she has lost the truest model of love on which she thought she could always depend. That's why you need to redouble your efforts to ensure she knows she can always depend on you. Speak kindly of your former wife, positively of marriage, lovingly to your daughter, and hopefully about love itself.

Rae Anne's Reality Check

Married couples fight. Happy, loving, and passionate married couples fight. I'm sure you already know this. I'm sure you are well versed in the area. Oftentimes a five-minute spat will be resolved quickly and laughed about with no further ramifications. But if your daughter hears you yelling—especially at a young age—it will be scarring to her. It doesn't matter what the argument is about or how quickly it ends; all that will matter is the fear she feels from hearing it. Your daughter is living with the reality that more than half the kids her age—her friends and classmates—have divorced parents. Forty percent are raised without their fathers. Divorce is an ever-present truth in her reality. She has friends with constantly packed suitcases, beds in two homes, and competing parental schedules. I say all of this so you know what is going through your daughter's mind when she hears Mom yelling at Dad and vice versa. So be smart. I know you can't control when fights happen, but maybe you can control how loud they get and where they happen. Maybe knowing that your young daughter is down the hall is enough to have you stop the fighting all together. Maybe when things get out of hand, afterward as a united couple you can talk to her about it and the resolution. I don't know. But this is just me, someone raised in a very happy home, telling you what it's like to hear your happy and loving parents fight. It cuts you deeply, instills fear, and makes you question everything. Do what you can to limit that kind of stress on your daughter.

About My Dad

Clearly you have purchased this book and read at least this chapter, so you are putting some stock into what my father has to say. He is a pretty smart man, with a few good anecdotes and lessons up his sleeve, so I can understand why. But when I look at my father, that's who I see: my dad. With all his flaws and gifts and motivations. And that man needs Rita. I have no doubt in my mind that my mom makes him a better man, the man whose kids are turning out okay and whose books you want to read. She challenges him and empowers him. Respects him and loves him. She pushes him to be a good father and a good man. So look at your wife. She is raising this little girl with you; she is fighting the fight right alongside you. She has flaws and gifts just as you do. Hopefully you bring out the best in each other. The best way you can give your daughter the best dad is to partner with your wife to be the best husband and let her help you become the best man. Isn't that how families work? Humble yourself enough to know you can do better, and count on your bride to take you to that next level.

"As is the mother, so is her daughter."

—Ezekiel 16:44 KJV

CHAPTER FIVE

Your Daughter and This Fallen World

*Our problem is not to be rid of fear but rather to
harness and master it.*

—*Martin Luther King Jr.*

If your little girl is under the age of three, you can skip this
chapter for now. Instead, just keep doing what comes naturally.
Love on her. Tickle her. Burble her tummy. Play peek-a-boo and
give horsey rides. Let her climb up onto your lap and nuzzle into
your chest. Enjoy every moment. Expect great things for your little
girl and be wonderfully optimistic for the future. Let your words
and actions give her confidence that grace and beauty can be found
around every corner.

Yes, we live in an uncertain world. For your daughter's sake,
you'll want to stay informed and vigilant. But your primary goal is
to work on your relationship. That's your best strategy for protecting her from falling prey to the avalanche of lies and temptations
waiting for her out there.

For as long as possible, allow her to be a little girl. As her daddy,
you have the unique responsibility to protect her from what lies

ahead. The upcoming generation faces challenges and decisions never confronted by baby boomers, Gen X, or millennials. Technology, media bias, global influences, and the redefinition of family will challenge every long-established social and moral code. Thankfully, your daughter has a father ready and willing to prepare her to stand up for a better way.

For now, help her enjoy and even bask in her current stage of life. Soon enough, you'll be called to arm yourself for battle on her behalf. That means you need to stay on top of news and trends, gather tools and resources, enlist allies, and know your enemy.

Today, even the most vigilant fathers can no longer hold back the onslaught of cultural forces. But what you can do is come alongside your daughter and help equip her to make her own wise choices and even stand up for herself in battle. That day may come sooner than you think.

Insight for GirlDads: Let Fear Motivate You

I probably don't have to, but allow me to list a few things that dads dwell on when they lie awake and think about their daughters. Teenage pregnancy. Sexually transmitted diseases. Abortion. Date rape. Peer pressure. Abduction. Sexting. Sexual promiscuity. Cutting. Mean girls. Cults. Gender confusion. Anorexia. Bulimia. Suicide. Addictions. Alcohol abuse. Pornography. Drunk driving.

You may mistakenly think some of these perils are limited to boys, but that's another example of our changing culture. Exposure to pornography, for example, has increased significantly among teen girls, leading to addiction, corrupted attitudes about sex, and debilitating shame.

Scared yet? That feeling may not be a bad thing. There's both value in and benefits to healthy fear. To some, fear may be paralyzing, but may I suggest you accept it as empowering. Let fear remind you to be prepared for whatever threatens you and your family. That's when a dad's truest purpose comes out. That's when you are called upon to "Be on your guard; stand firm in the faith; be courageous; be strong" (1 Corinthians 16:13).

Jesus told His disciples, "Peace I leave with you; my peace I give you. I do not give to you as the world gives. Do not let your hearts be troubled and do not be afraid" (John 14:27).

The peace of knowing Christ is closely related to a kind of fear that's actually desirable: the awe and respect for God. Psalm 111:10 confirms "The fear of the LORD is the beginning of wisdom; all who follow his precepts have good understanding." That's a valuable, life-affirming fear that equips and motivates.

Insight for GirlDads: Enlist Virtuous Allies

If you do encounter fear that steals your peace and keeps you up at night regarding your daughter's welfare, then you'll want to enlist additional help from people in your sphere of influence who care about her, too. This is not a campaign you need to wage by yourself. As mentioned in the previous chapter, your daughter's mom should be a primary partner in this battle. Also grandparents, aunts, uncles, and your daughter's older siblings and cousins. Friends and neighbors. Pastors and youth pastors. Teachers, coaches, and guidance counselors. Don't forget, the parents of your daughter's friends may be having the same concerns. Get to know them—not to gang up on your daughter, but to take stock of the resources available to you as challenges mount.

Even people you've never met care about your daughter and can be a valuable resource for information and cultural acumen. That includes authors, speakers, and even musicians and entertainers. Of course, there may very well be more media influencers out there who are working *against* you than with you—which only reinforces your need to engage like-minded allies.

One goal is to stay informed regarding what's going on in the world in general and, more specifically, in your daughter's world. You can't possibly know everything your preteen or teenage daughter is going through, but you don't want to live in denial.

Don't think of these allies as spies, tattletales, or narcs. That suggests that you're at war *with* your daughter. You, your daughter, and all these men and women are on the same side. It's not about speculation or spreading gossip. You're really simply building relationships and opening doors of communication.

In other words, you are not alone in this battle for your daughter's physical and spiritual welfare. Plus, there is one more powerful resource you may not have considered: your daughter herself.

Insight for GirlDads: Your Daughter May Be Part of the Solution

Because you have been providing her with love and guidance for more than a decade, your teenage daughter may be stronger than you give her credit for. Don't let your guard down, but you would be wise to work toward standing shoulder to shoulder with her in this battle against the evil one. Your little girl may very well have a clear and strategic view of Satan's tricks and tools. That long list of fatherhood fears listed above? If your daughter is an active participant in life, she has seen them firsthand. All of them. That's a sad fact, but it should also serve as encouragement to you.

As she matures, proactively open the door to real-life adult conversations. Ask how she would—and how she has—handled some of life's challenges. In recent years, Rae Anne and I have talked about a few things she has seen firsthand that frighten me more than a little. Amazingly, she has responded to these situations with wisdom and courage beyond her years. My reaction? I'm more than a little impressed at her strength and savvy. (I'm also a little glad I didn't know about it at the time.) Of course, Rae Anne can come to me with any concern in any crisis. But there's great satisfaction in seeing her successfully take on challenges of life without needing to be rescued by her old man.

I pray your daughter is also well-prepared and increasingly confident, and that she is also a positive influence on friends and colleagues.

Insight for GirlDads: Perfect Love Drives Out Fear

You love your daughter. Your love is strong, vibrant, and unconditional. But it's not perfect. God's love is. And you'll be glad to know it "drives out fear" (1 John 4:18).

Early and often make sure your daughter understands and experiences God's perfect, empowering love. When she accepts that love, you need never live in fear of her eternal destination. When it comes to my own daughter, Rae Anne, I have that confidence. But that doesn't mean the work of earthly fathers is done. We have also been given the responsibility to protect our families and help prepare them for opportunities to fulfill God's call in their lives here on Earth.

Insight for GirlDads: Wield the Right Weapons against the World

Use the dangers of the world as motivation to stay close, involved, and informed. Your weapons are truth, love, righteousness, mercy, and justice.

With love, remind your daughter often of how valuable, beautiful, and cherished she is. With truth, warn her of the presence of evil and how Satan seeks to steal and destroy. With righteousness *and humility*, help her discern wrong from right. With mercy, hear her perspective, and be slow and thoughtful in your responses. When she makes bad choices, with discernment and justice, respond with a balance of grace and reasonable consequence.

Don't make the mistake of so many fathers who are not prepared to fight for the hearts and minds of their daughters. They heedlessly wish away the demons or, worse, don't believe demons exist. Even dads who do have a battle plan often dangerously underestimate the power of the enemy.

Knowing the dangers your daughter faces and fiercely protecting her through her teenage years and well into her twenties will go a long way toward opening doors to the joy-filled life God has waiting for her.

Insight for GirlDads: Satan's Latest Attack on Young Women

The best current evidence of our fallen world is the invasive nature and onslaught of social media. For your daughter, it never ends.

Especially right around the transition to high school, your daughter will be overwhelmed with hormonal changes, cultural expectations, body-image issues, peer pressure, and other exhausting concerns. For your generation and those preceding it, most girls could count on evenings at home when they could still be a little girl. Family time meant rest and respite. The truth is, even those older teenage girls who declare they want to go out every night are really just succumbing to outside pressure. They may not even realize it, but all girls welcome the time to stop putting on an act for the world.

The need for rest has long been built into the human condition. Even God rested on the seventh day of creation (Genesis 2:2). The Ten Commandments call for a Sabbath. Jesus promises "rest for your souls." Unfortunately, for our daughters, rest is in short supply. Because of the constancy of social media, there's no time when their hearts can be still and anxiety can abate.

For the first time in human history, there are no breaks. No silence, which is so necessary to dream dreams and think deep thoughts. The constant attention demanded by screens and phones is stealing the imagination and innocence of our girls (and boys). It's impossible for them to follow the instruction of Psalm 46:10 to "Be still, and know that I am God."

In Luke 10:38–42, we see why Satan loves busyness. When Jesus visited two sisters, Mary sat at his feet, listening to His every word, while Martha was distracted by cultural expectations. Jesus said, "Martha, Martha, you are worried and upset about many things, but few things are needed—or indeed only one. Mary has chosen what is better, and it will not be taken away from her."

That lesson is one all dads need to take to heart and share with our daughters. Jesus called Martha to task for being distracted by the preoccupation to serve. How much more tragic is it when our daughters are being distracted by the preoccupation to post, text, and tweet?

Insight for GirlDads: Never Give Up on Her

You are not responsible for your daughter's actions. Especially as she moves toward adulthood, you have to accept the fact that she will make some unhealthy choices. (You made a few mistakes in your own youth, remember?) Your challenge—the balancing act—is to know when to rescue her and when to let natural consequences take their course. Maybe she should fail a class because she cheated on the mid-term exam. Maybe she should be kicked off the soccer team for breaking the high school sports code of conduct. It's difficult to imagine, but maybe she should even spend a night in jail.

But she's still your daughter. You still love her without condition. When the world crashes in, you want to open your arms, but not necessarily take all the steps she wants you to take. In general, hiring a lawyer to battle the school board is a bad idea. In general, when she totals her car, it may not be a good idea to instantly buy her a new one. Helping her out with one month's rent is probably okay. But not month after month after month.

Get on the same page as your daughter's mother, and then have the hard talk or hard talks. Make room in your heart and home (if necessary). But set parameters and expectations. The sooner, the better.

Here's a general principle. If the consequences threaten her health or long-term well-being, then rescue. If the consequences teach her a much-needed lesson which she should have learned long ago, then step back. For example, don't let her spend a night in a big city lockup. But several hours behind bars in a local small town police station might be an excellent wake-up call.

All that being said, please remember: Even in the worst circumstance, your goal is still to pull her toward you, not push her away.

Insight for GirlDads: We're Not Home Yet

When tragedy strikes and all seems hopeless, there is still reason to take heart. This world is not our home. Before your daughter leaves your influence, make sure she understands the Gospel. We all have sinned, which separates us from God. One way or another, the penalty of sin must be paid. Astonishingly, Jesus paid that price on your daughter's behalf. It's a free gift from a loving God, and all she has to do is believe it and receive it. With that understanding and by accepting that grace, your daughter has a spot reserved in eternity, leaving behind this broken world.

Rae Anne's Reality Check

The world is a broken and terrifying place. You will be tempted to try and protect your pure and innocent daughter from all the dangers of things outside your home. But the fact is, one day she will leave your protection and become a citizen of the world. On that day, you do not want her to be blindsided by the darkness; you want her to be well-equipped to fight it. And even overcome it. While the Church and Christian friends are good and important things for your daughter to have, I believe it is just as important to have non-believing friends and to spend time in the secular world. It is especially important for her to experience these things while you can be there to help guide her through them.

Raising a daughter oblivious to the brokenness of the world will not only put her in danger, but will also leave her ineffective as a tool in the fight for good. You cannot expect victory in the battle against evil or work to build the Kingdom if you do not understand the enemy. In the Garden of Gethsemane the night before He was crucified, Jesus prayed for the future of His disciples and those who would follow Him in the future.

> "My prayer is not that you take them out of the world but that you protect them from the evil one. They are not of the world, even as I am not of it. Sanctify them by the truth; your word is truth. As you sent me into the world, I have sent them into the world." (John 17:15–18)

You'll note that Jesus did not say, "I send them to stay in their small Christian communities" or "I send them to live in the comfort of their own churches alongside friends who will not challenge or question them." He sends us out into a world that hates us and will try to destroy us. That is the mandate of the Great Commission.

You should be helping equip your daughter with the sword of the Spirit, the belt of truth, and the full armor of God described in Ephesians 6 so she will be able to fight this battle. I have honestly seen many times someone I knew growing up in church who was protected in their Christian school, with their Christian friends, in their Christian churches, and the moment they left their Christian colleges, the world swallowed them whole. When that happens, I often wonder how the results would have been different if that individual had been empowered to fight, rather than shielded from the enemy and this fallen world.

So empower your daughter. Equip her. Give her the tools to survive in the world and beat the enemy and show her how to use them. Because, whether you like it or not, she will be on her own one day—and just like sharpening her skates before her hockey game or helping her prep for her mock trial case, you may not be able to do the work for her, but how you have prepared her may make all the difference.

Hey, Rae Anne . . .

My daughter is constantly getting into trouble at school, and recently she had a run-in with the police. She's not some common criminal, but I keep having to bail her out of trouble, and I fear she is getting worse.

It sounds like your daughter is testing boundaries. Her own boundaries: how far can she take things and how disobedient does she want to be? Your boundaries: how far can she push you and when will you stop rescuing her? Society's boundaries: how much can she get away with and what are the actual repercussions?

As hard as it might be to admit, you probably are hurting her by bailing her out all the time, rather than helping her. It's true that kids make mistakes—and when it is genuinely a one-time mistake, you probably want to be there to help clean it up. But sometimes you have to let your daughter face the music. In this case, it seems her actions are purposeful, calculated, and recurrent. Since she knows you will clean it up for her, she doesn't really concern herself with the size of the mess. So next time, don't save her. Now, if it is a matter of safety, never put her in danger. If you allow her to spend a night in jail, you may want to spend the night sleeping on a bench in the police station lobby. The idea is that when she begins to feel the full weight of her consequences, you want to be there to control the burn. For example, wouldn't you rather have her suffer a school suspension than a jail sentence?

Let your daughter know your tolerance for her behavior has a limit. If you can, go ahead and define that limit. Then stick to it. Let her fall flat on her face now, while you are still available to clean her wounds and minimize the long-term damage. She may be angry because you didn't bail her out sooner. At that point, she needs to grasp the concept that you can't and won't always be there, and the repercussions are only going to get more severe and longer-lasting. It is also vital that she understand that while there are limits to your ability to rescue her, there are no limits to your love or your forgiveness.

Hey, Rae Anne . . .

My daughter did something that I cannot believe she would do. She has apologized and repented, but I don't think I can trust her again.

In these kinds of scenarios, there are four players involved: love, trust, respect, and forgiveness. It's possible to love someone without trusting them, respecting them, or even liking them. Think about your siblings growing up, your off-putting uncle or annoying cousin. You love them but that's about it. You still love your daughter. I know this because you wouldn't be reading this book or asking the question if you didn't. You love her, and that is why she was able to hurt you so deeply. So first, remember this love and don't stop telling your daughter that you love her.

But trust and respect are in a different category. Those two things are not rights, but earned privileges. Go ahead and tell your daughter she has broken your heart and that the trust and respect you once had for her is damaged and cannot be easily fixed. Then give her the chance to rebuild.

Even if it takes years of struggle and enormous effort, the chance for a renewed trust and respect must be offered. Which brings us to forgiveness. Forgiveness is a painful activity, especially when someone so dear to you is the affronter. It may help to remember how you were desperate for forgiveness from God, how you repented, and how you were given forgiveness you did not deserve. Forgive as God has forgiven you. If your daughter truly repents and asks for your grace, you need to give it to her. You can acknowledge how she hurt you and how it is a struggle for you to forgive, but at the end of the day, make sure your arms are open.

We live in a broken world, and your daughter will succumb to its brokenness at some point. If you are on the receiving end of some pain she may have caused you, use it as an opportunity to teach her about the power of forgiveness, the strength of your love, the fragile nature of trust and respect, and the reality of consequences.

Rae Anne's Reality Check

Your daughter has questions you do not want to answer. Questions about war, death, world hunger, hate, racism, mental health, terrorism, pain, sexism, etc. Questions you have struggled with yourself in your own mind and heart. When these topics arise, there are two key things you should do.

First, be honest with her. Of course, her age will determine the details and your wording choices. Tell her the truth the best you know how and be willing to research and learn together the answers you're not sure of. If your daughter is perceptive enough to be asking questions about these things, then she is probably perceptive enough to know if you're lying and strong enough to handle the honest answer. Also know that as we live in the age of the internet, if you are not honest with her, she will find someone honest (or not so honest) to discuss them with on the world wide web. Who would you rather have shaping your daughter's view of the world?

The second thing you need to be is brokenhearted about the world. When she asks you questions about human trafficking, genocide, or terrorism, you should make your emotions clear on the matter. If you're angry, be angry; if you're sad be sad; if you're confused, be confused. Be genuine. Because if you are genuine, then she is given license to be genuine with you. Honest, genuine, and vulnerable conversations will build and strengthen your relationship, so do not shy away from the awkward or upsetting topics.

"Parents can only give good advice or put them on the right paths, but the final forming of a person's character lies in their own hands."

—Anne Frank

"As a father has compassion on his children, so the LORD has compassion on those who fear him."

—Psalm 103:13

CHAPTER SIX

Your Daughter's Brokenness

Depression is the inability to construct a future.

—Rollo May

In some respects, I have no right to write this chapter. It's about how to respond when your daughter is suffering from emotional, physical, psychological, and/or spiritual damage.

The women in my family—including my beautiful wife, my astute daughter, my four wonderful daughters-in-law, and my two perfect young granddaughters—are doing quite well. At least, I think so.

I'm not naïve. There are certainly challenges—past, present, and future—in everyone's life. Still, as of this writing, I can confirm that, while there have been a few health issues along the way and some life disappointments, these women and girls I love so much have not had to endure any long illnesses or hospital stays, bouts of depression, substance abuse, or mental illness. Looking at our family, most people would say we're doing pretty well and have been more than fortunate. I would have to agree.

There's a high probability I'm overlooking or forgetting something. Like all dads, I've undoubtedly fallen short in this area. Admittedly, my natural optimism and focus on the future occasionally clouds my cognition. Still, I can affirm that all three generations of Payleitner females are strong and healthy in mind, body, and spirit—which is why my credentials to address "Your Daughter's Brokenness" from direct personal experience are open for debate. However, my coauthor Rae Anne insisted we include this chapter, mostly because she knows more than a few girls who are hurting . . . desperately. Rae Anne also knows that—in many cases—the fathers of those young women typically don't say or do the right thing at the right time.

Having spoken and interacted with thousands of dads, I am also aware of the extent of personal brokenness in our world—especially with men agonizing over how to respond to their daughters, who are scared, angry, lost, or feeling unloved and worthless. I've been invited into the inner circle of families in crisis, and I've seen what works—and what doesn't.

Is your daughter broken? Is she headed that direction? Here are a few insights I've learned from other dads, professional counselors, medical professionals, teachers, government officials, qualified researchers, and Scripture.

Insight for GirlDads: Crud Happens

Fathers tend to blame themselves when a daughter goes off the deep end or suffers a personal tragedy. Please don't. Depression, mental illness, anger, suicidal thoughts, and deep sorrow can visit any family at any time. Accidents happen. Physical ailments such as leukemia, brain tumors, cardiac conditions, fibromyalgia, and so on typically occur without warning. Non-professionals may suggest that issues like acne, obesity, anorexia, bulimia, sleep disorders, broken hearts, and anxiety are somehow controllable or avoidable. Those short-sighted judgments are inaccurate and potentially damaging. Also, please remember that sexually transmitted diseases, unwanted pregnancy, drug overdoses, and alcohol poisoning can ravage a teenage girl's well-being following one brief and bad decision.

Dad, I know you would like to protect your daughter from every bit of pain and sorrow, but there will always exist circumstances beyond your control. In your head, you may agonize over choices you made or signals you may have overlooked. But please don't beat yourself up. Instead, use your role as a loving father to motivate yourself to address the problem with wisdom and determination. If you spiral into your own torrent of guilt or shame, you will not be much help to your little girl, who needs you right now. Okay?

Insight for GirlDads: If Your Daughter Is Ill, Find a Doctor

You won't find any medical advice in this book except that your daughter should have regular visits with a trusted physician. Almost certainly, before she leaves your loving care, your daughter will face issues requiring medical treatment or perhaps a licensed psychologist. But the truth is that some families live in denial or fear when it comes to doctors. There's a long list of symptoms that should trigger a visit to a doctor, including sleeplessness, sudden weight loss, anxiety, an irregular menstrual cycle, memory loss, or severe headaches. It's not sexist to say your daughter's mother should probably take the lead on many of these concerns. There are medical, emotional, and psychological issues you would find difficult to grasp. You can help by being quietly supportive and making sure your medical insurance is up to date.

The other side of this issue is that some girls like the attention of trips to the emergency room. Or every minor symptom is cause for panic, because the young lady might not grasp the natural healing process of the human body. Not every headache is a brain tumor. Not every stomachache is a burst appendix. If that describes your daughter, that might also be a discussion you'll want to have with a professional.

Insight for GirlDads: Decide If There Really Is a Problem

Let's say your teenage daughter has made some noticeable changes in recent weeks. She has shut down lines of communications. She begins to dress weirdly. Her grades drop a bit. She has a new set of friends. She quits one or two of her favorite extracurricular activities. She stops talking about college and starts talking about taking some time off after high school. There may be reasonable reasons to be concerned. Panic, however, is not your best option.

Again, you've ruled out any illness. What you may have is a daughter who is just trying to figure out who she is and what she wants. For as long as she can remember, you have been making all her decisions. At some point, she realizes that her goal of eventual independence requires some original thought and self-reliance. That's a good instinct. But it also means there will be—there should be—a season in which your daughter moves *away* from your direct influence.

So how do you know if the pendulum is swinging too far?

This is one of those times that you'll be glad you have a wife with whom you can communicate. Someone who loves your daughter as much as you do and can either confirm your suspicions or explain what she is going through because she went through the same thing herself two or three decades ago. If your daughter's mother is not around, you're going to have to quadruple your effort to stay on top of the situation.

Use every resource available. Talk to other parents. Look for clues. Especially track changes in behavior that have a dark side. Keep a private journal of things that don't seem right. Is there money missing from your wallet? Do cell phones go unanswered? Have you caught your daughter lying right to your face? When you look in her eyes, is your little girl still there? When you compare notes with your daughter's mother, what patterns do you discover?

If your concern continues to grow, widen your search by including other people who love your daughter. Identify other caring adults in her life such as teachers, coaches, neighbors, youth pastors, and the parents of her longtime friends. Maybe include your daughter's siblings. This may feel like you're ganging up on her, but it's just the opposite. You're gathering a team to support, pray for, and perhaps be part of an intervention for your daughter. The goal is to not make false accusations. The goal is to gather facts.

Insight for GirlDads: Celebrate Her Defiance

Remember how cute it was when your three-year-old daughter told you she didn't want pickle relish on her hot dog? It was a clear act of rebellion. Up until that point, she liked pickle relish, but suddenly she was asserting her personal authority. You delighted in her personal resolve and were smart enough not to argue. Your little maverick got her hot dog her way.

A few years later, there will be other personal choices you don't see coming. Maybe even some with which you disagree. But just maybe, they're the exact right choice for your daughter. Examples: Quitting tennis. Trying out for lacrosse. Joining the Army. Starting a band. Wearing no makeup. Wearing too much makeup. Changing high schools. Not going on the family vacation this summer. Painting her bedroom without permission. Going vegan.

We're talking about personal choices, not moral values or legal concerns. Be clear and steadfast on issues of right and wrong. Intervene or overrule, if needed. But make room for personal choices that happen to be different than the ones you might make.

Expressed another way, you don't want your daughter to do only stuff that you approve of. If she spends her teenage years acting like a perfect angel who is constantly seeking your validation, there's a good chance she's going to experiment with some devilish behavior when she's not under your direct authority. Way too many good kids who blindly followed Mom and Dad's rules through high school turn into party animals when they head off to college or out into the world.

So . . . if it's basically harmless, *celebrate* those times when her choices don't make sense to you.

Insight for GirlDads: Each Generation Will Push the Envelope

One summer, my dad overreacted to something my older sister did, and even I knew it was no big deal. It was the 1970s. The station wagon was packed for our annual trip up north to the cottage on Pine Lake. As Mary Kay walked out into the driveway, the sun reflecting off her hair revealed she had recently tinted it with a slight red hue. Normally soft-spoken, my dad went a little crazy. "Mary Kay, what did you do to yourself? Margie, how could you let this happen!" Well, my seventeen-year-old sister instantly went into defense mode. "Dad, it's no big deal!" My mom tried to explain that really, "It's only temporary." My brother, my little sister, and I wondered if our vacation was about to be canceled.

The car was a little quiet the first hour of the drive. As the trip unfolded, my dad settled down, and our vacation was not spoiled by my sister's radical act of hair-coloring defiance. I don't know if my dad ever apologized for his outburst, and I'm not sure he needed to. For the record, in the years that followed, my sisters and my mother all colored their hair multiple times.

How does that scene play out in this generation? Compared to some of the decisions your daughter has made or will make, a barely noticeable hair coloring is pretty tame. So let's ask, "What would cause a father to overreact today?" Is it multiple piercings? A little shoulder butterfly tattoo? A giant face tattoo? Or maybe some dramatic declaration that turns your world upside down?

Like my own father, you may initially go a little crazy. If that begins to happen, try to minimize the damage. Don't keep exploding. Don't say things you'll regret. Don't cancel your vacation or ignore the needs of the rest of the family. Rather than push your daughter away, it might be the exact right time to come together as a family. Because when the dust settles, you still want to be a family, right?

Insight for GirlDads: Retain the Right to Speak into Her Life

For generations, fathers and daughters have been trying to figure each other out. Sometimes that leads to words we regret, decisions made with insufficient information, slammed doors, lost years, and even tears of anguish at funerals because reconciliation never came.

But reconciliation and joy are really only a conversation away. While time does heal most wounds, I still recommend that you pursue some kind of common ground and harmony sooner rather than later.

Even if she's been intentionally ticking you off. Even if she punches you in the gut with the words, "I hate you!" Even if you don't know what to say or do anymore. Keep pulling her toward you. Don't push her away. If she takes three steps away, take two steps toward her. If she slams her bedroom door, wait a few minutes, then knock gently. Even if she doesn't respond, go ahead and say, "Chloe, I hate it when we argue. I love you so much. We really do need to keep talking about this. If there's something I can do for you, let me know." And, Dad, if there's some kind of apology you need to give because you spoke harshly or lost your cool, do that as soon as the opportunity presents itself.

Insight for GirlDads: When She Forgets Who She Is

Your family name stands for something. Maybe it's your fun-loving spirit. Maybe it's your patriotism, athleticism, leadership, community service. Maybe your family has seen generations of teachers, builders, politicians, artists, or spiritual leaders. Yet suddenly, your maturing daughter seems to have turned her back on her heritage and life purpose. As her father, your gut reaction is to think, *Where did I go wrong?*

You think she's broken, but she's not. Really, she's testing. Testing her own talents and beliefs. Testing the rules and beliefs she has learned from you. Testing what her friends and teachers say.

You could even call it spreading her wings and seeing the best way to fly.

Dad, if you really want her to be a success in life, she has to go through that exercise. God has prepared work for her, and she needs to figure out what that is. Ephesians 2:10 is clear: "For we are God's handiwork, created in Christ Jesus to do good works, which God prepared in advance for us to do."

From a spiritual perspective, this is also a good thing. Even if you wholeheartedly raised her under loving biblical guidelines, she can't depend on your faith for guidance or salvation. Your little girl has to make her own decision to follow Christ. That's the only way she will gain the counsel of the Holy Spirit or receive the grace Jesus won on the cross.

As a matter of fact, your daughter's testing may be a sign of maturity. First Thessalonians 5:21–22 (NLT) tells us, "Test everything that is said. Hold on to what is good. Stay away from every kind of evil." To really own her faith, she has to wrestle with the big questions.

With all that in mind, your little girl needs you to make sure she hears the great truths and steers clear of the darker forces of the world. That's your job, Dad, and as you already know, the best strategy is to begin early and continue sharing your wisdom and experience as you do life together. Heed the advice of Deuteronomy 6:6–7:

> These commandments that I give you today are to be on
> your hearts. Impress them on your children. Talk about
> them when you sit at home and when you walk along the
> road, when you lie down and when you get up.

Insight for GirlDads: Maybe Ransack Her Room

Your daughter trusts you. You've spent a lifetime building that trust, and you shouldn't take it lightly. However, if you suspect your daughter is engaging in an activity that may endanger her well-being, you have the right and responsibility to get the truth. As a matter of fact, she *trusts* you to intervene. That might mean ransacking her room.

If her life or health is in danger, you need to have the courage to empty dresser drawers, overturn mattresses, reach behind books, open every shoebox on every shelf, and go through pockets of jeans thrown on the floor.

I pray you don't have to resort to such drastic actions. You can be sure that your investigation will result in a loud and painful confrontation. For a season following your invasion of her privacy, she will close you out and leave you scared and brokenhearted. But if she's doing damage to herself and if you really love her (and I know you do), then get the proof and get some help.

No matter what your search uncovers, you should expect that you and your family are going to need some face-to-face time with a counselor, doctor, or pastor. Seeking professional help may feel like you've somehow failed as a father. But just the opposite is true. Exposing dark corners of your home to the light of truth is a courageous act and requires strength and fearlessness that doesn't come easily even to the most determined men.

The Bible promises that our job is to shine God's truth on any and all dark secrets and He will do the rest.

> Have nothing to do with the fruitless deeds of darkness,
> but rather expose them. It is shameful even to mention

what the disobedient do in secret. But everything exposed by the light becomes visible—and everything that is illuminated becomes a light. (Ephesians 5:11–13)

Through this entire ordeal, I urge you to maintain high expectations and steadfast hope. Yes, you can expect weeks or months of anger, denial, and separation. Expect to miss your little girl. Expect to have your own set of regrets and feelings of guilt. But also expect to walk through this dark storm and find healing on the other side.[1]

Insight for GirlDads: God Is Still God

If you feel helpless because your daughter is hurting and it seems like there's nothing you can do, it's really okay to be angry at God. He can take it. As a matter of fact, when you find yourself in despair, He's closer than ever, waiting for you to turn to Him. One of my favorite psalms promises, "The LORD is close to the brokenhearted and saves those who are crushed in spirit. The righteous person may have many troubles, but the Lord delivers him from them all; he protects all his bones, not one of them will be broken" (Psalm 34:18–20).

Talk things over with God. Let Him help you sort out your options. He will deliver you—*and* that little girl who will always have a piece of your heart. On behalf of your entire family—especially your daughter—surrender your own human agenda. Trust that on the other side of this traumatic and painful season, God's lovingkindness will open the door for you to become a family again. Call it a victory in Christ. Expect to be united by love, mutual appreciation, and a sense of amazement that God can use the crud of this world to bring you closer than ever.

THINGS TO LOOK FORWARD TO

Whatever you're going through right now—harsh words, communication blackout, fear, guilt, anger, detachment—don't give up on the future. There are no guarantees of reconciliation, but there is hope. Dad, grab onto a fresh vision of you and your daughter a few weeks, a few months, or a few years from now.

- Taking her out for coffee for no reason
- Cuddling up on the couch watching a classic movie
- Moving her into a college dorm
- That photo of the two of you when she's wearing a cap and gown
- Your daughter asking your advice about a problem at work
- Taking her out for dinner to celebrate her new job, a promotion, an opening night, a presidential appointment, a million-dollar signing bonus, an early parole, or a year's sobriety
- Hearing her tell you she's found the man she wants to marry
- Walking her down the aisle
- Spending way too much money on her wedding
- Grandkids!
- Taking your grandkids to ballgames, pumpkin patches, and carnivals
- Your daughter caring for you in your old age
- Your daughter joining you in Heaven

Rae Anne's Reality Check

My father was being absolutely honest when he said I made him write this chapter. I had to twist his arm a little because he couldn't seem to find the anecdotes from his own life that typically spur his writing. He is—as I am—fully aware of how good we have it, how blessed we are as a family.

But this chapter needed to be written because—as your daughter's father—you need to know how broken life can be. Maybe you come from a broken life yourself, or maybe you were fortunate enough that unrelenting personal darkness never reached your doorway. Either way, when you held your daughter in your arms for the first time, I know you promised to give her a perfect life and protect her from every hardship or boogey monster. But this chapter is not about robbers breaking into your home or tornadoes requiring you to take shelter, or anything so black and white. This is about your need to admit there are things out of your control. Illness, both physical and mental, death that will destroy her world, pain she won't share with you, and pain she will share with you that you cannot do anything about.

It is important to know that no matter how much you love her or how impenetrable the walls are you build around her, your daughter will get hurt. She may even get a little broken. And you may not even realize it. This reality check may be hard to swallow or, as you hold that little girl in your arms, you may refuse to believe it. But a degree of brokenness is a reality at some point for just about every girl. Even if your daughter is healthy and happy while in your home, she will see brokenness in her friends or struggle with battles herself when she leaves your protection. Be prepared. Be a little scared. But always be there.

Hey, Rae Anne . . .

I think my adult daughter is struggling with drug/alcohol abuse. I feel powerless.

In a lot of ways, you *are* powerless. If your daughter is an adult and independent from you, there is very little power you hold over her. But power should not be the goal here. The goal should be to help your daughter regain her health, hope, and sobriety.

Drug and alcohol abuse tends to travel a route that makes a stop only at rock bottom. If your daughter comes to you before that inevitable fall asking for your help to get into rehab or to help her recover, obviously jump at the chance. But more likely, she will come to you for money or a place to stay. What is important in that moment is that when you have that leverage over her, use it for her betterment. Don't pay her rent, pay for her rehab. Don't give her cash, take her grocery shopping. If and when she does hit that rock bottom, be there to cushion her so it doesn't destroy her. It will be messy, painful, and probably expensive, but this is the fight of any parent.

You may have to use ultimatums like, "I will give you some-place to stay if you go to rehab." But steer clear of ultimatums such as, "If you don't go to rehab you are not allowed into my house again." Be firm and strong for her own sake, but do not put love on the table. She has to know that you love her in her darkest moment, and always will.

Yes, you will get angry and frustrated, hurt and sad. If your daughter is battling addiction, it is a lifelong battle of an illness, and it will be a lifelong battle for you as well. The best advice I can give you is to make sure that you are caring for yourself too. Just as there are programs for those suffering from addiction, there are also programs for people who love those with addictions. Make sure your whole family is getting the resources they need. Refer to your local Al-Anon and Alateen groups, as well as some variations that may meet at a local church. Find a community of support, and you will be better equipped to support your daughter.

Turn the medical and psychological issues over to experts; you just need to be her father. Be there. Love her.

Rae Anne's Reality Check

If you need to ransack your daughter's room—as my father articulated above—don't do it while she's out of the house in an attempt to catch her off guard. Instead, sit her down, explain to her why you have to do this, specify the mutual trust she has broken, and then give her the chance to start building that trust up again, maybe by surrendering the shoplifted merchandise or drugs to you upfront. If not, let her stand there while you tear apart her room.

Whenever possible, you should be the beacon of calm and reason. If you are calm and reasonable, the chance of her matching that tone is far more likely. The same goes for yelling and slamming doors.

Hey, Rae Anne . . .

I think my daughter is suffering from anxiety and/or depression. I don't know what to do. Where do I begin?

If you yourself have not struggled with mental illness or emotional imbalance, it will be nearly impossible for you to relate to your daughter's struggles. So don't try. The worst possible thing you can do is belittle the battle your daughter is fighting or think you can paper over the issues with easy answers. I can guarantee there are already people in her life, from her close friends to teachers to the media, that have already done that. People she trusts have minimized her suffering, calling her "crazy" or "dramatic."

Please do not pretend to know what she is going through. Imagine you were fighting stomach cancer and someone (even a well-intentioned someone) equated it to indigestion or the stomach flu. She doesn't need you to know her pain; she needs you to acknowledge it and get her the help she needs.

If your daughter tells you she believes she is a suffering from mental illness or some other struggle, ask her why she thinks so, and listen. Then take her to your family physician and continue the conversation. Include other professionals as recommended. Medications may be part of the solution, but start with engaging hard questions in a safe space. You'd be surprised how quickly someone suffering will open up once they are asked about it by someone they trust.

Once your daughter is in treatment, and perhaps diagnosed, then make it your job to become a student of her illness. Read articles, ask questions of her doctors, be aware. But again, realize that you do not know what it is to be her, to fight her battles, and to struggle as she struggles. So don't pretend you do. Your best course of action is availability, personal vulnerability, and a commitment for the long haul.

Rae Anne's Reality Check

Even if you do not think that adverse mental health is actively affecting your daughter—or better yet, if your daughter is still in the baby/toddler phase—I strongly encourage you to become a student of basic mental illness warning signs and suicidal indicators. I am not qualified to list them here, but I encourage you to seek out these resources yourself. Start with your child's school or your physician. With every passing generation, these issues become more prominent, the consequences more deadly, and it is our job to be a part of the solution.

Hey, Rae Anne . . .
My seventeen-year-old daughter has never given me any reason not to trust her. But I don't like the influence of one of her friends and I worry about what they do when I'm not there.
Do not break your daughter's trust. Hopefully with that trust you've built over the years comes a line of communication and mutual respect. Be careful; tread lightly. Once trust is broken with any individual, it's hard to restore. But your daughter's trust is especially sacred. That being said, your daughter's safety and well-being need to be a high priority as well. If you genuinely believe your daughter is beginning to take steps down some sort of dark path, the first thing you should do is ask her. It's a simple idea that a lot of frightened parents avoid. Instead, they accuse. They argue. They give ultimatums. They set artificial limits—all before having the facts or getting their daughter's side of the story. Your daughter might be the exact influence her friend needs; if you do trust her, she could be an amazing force for good among her peers.

Take advantage of your mutual trust and respect to sit down with her and have an honest conversation in which she feels free to be herself and tell you the truth. State your concerns calmly and give her a chance to explain. Find a way to discern the true nature of your daughter's dubious friends without making accusations. A lot of young people present a poor first impression, and hasn't your daughter earned the right to pick her friends? Don't let your rush to judgment break her trust. If you have these conversations early, before any problems arise, then the door is already open for further discussion—not to say, "I told you so," but to help her work through any challenge.

Now, if she shatters that trust by lying, sneaking out, or breaking household rules, confront her honestly. Be forthright with the fact that she has broken your trust in her. However, this does not give you the freedom to break her trust in you. Don't degrade yourself by acting like a teenager as well. The key here is preserving the mutual trust until she breaks it, having constant conversations.

"Rescue your hurting child at the top of any slippery slope."
—Jay Payleitner

"At sixteen, the adolescent knows about suffering because he himself has suffered, but he barely knows that other beings also suffer."
—Jean-Jacques Rousseau

CHAPTER SEVEN

Your Daughter's Boyfriends

*Watching your daughter being collected by her date
feels like handing over a million-dollar Stradivarius to
a gorilla.*

—Jim Bishop

Boys think about sex a lot. You already know that. That undeniable fact may be all the motivation you need to spend time with your daughter, treat her with dignity and respect, make yourself available to answer all her questions, and give her solid instruction on how to deal with those lecherous young male creatures who have but one thing on their mind.

But here's the challenge. You want your daughter—through her teenage years and beyond—to put up unmistakable signals that her body is off limits to impure thoughts and roving hands. However, you also want her to be taking good notes about the qualities she is looking for in a husband. If it's God's will, you want her eventually to find the right guy for her, settle down, and build a family.

You want her to have friends who are boys, but not be boy crazy. You want her to feel beautiful and even desirable, but not flaunt her sexuality or be a tease. You want her heart to be tender, but not easily broken. You want her to find true love and not be tricked by some guy who fakes love to get sex.

While much of this is way outside your control, Dad, there are things you can do. Truths you can teach. Warnings you can give. Doors you can open. And tears you can dry.

Insight for GirlDads: Get a Shotgun

Seriously? Well, you don't literally need to sit in a rocking chair on your front porch with a Winchester Model 21 across your lap. But when those young suitors start coming around, you need to be a visible force demonstrating an authentic determination to protect your precious daughter. Those hooligans need to know the girl they're courting has a dad who knows how valuable she is.

Don't scare them off. You do want them to come to your front door and ring your doorbell. You want those boys to shake your hand, so you can look them in the eye and size them up. If they're a little nervous, that's even better. It's the ones who are a little too sure of themselves who may attempt to sweet-talk your daughter into letting down her guard. Expect them to call you "sir." If your interrogation goes a little too far, that's actually a good thing. Your daughter might tell you later, "Daddy, you embarrassed Colin with all your questions." But really, she's glad you care.

Insight for GirlDads: Talk about God's Plan for Marriage

Let your daughter know that marriage—one man and one woman in a lifetime commitment—is a worthy goal. In an intentional conversation, explain that marriage is not a business relationship, legal contract, or a stage of life that happens for convenience or by accident. The second chapter in the Bible spells it out: "A man leaves his father and mother and is united to his wife, and they become one flesh" (Genesis 2:24).

What does it mean to "become one flesh"? Even if your daughter never asks that question, go ahead and answer it. And don't give a short answer. I believe God's instruction to become one flesh is a gift with multiple meanings and ramifications. That "bonding" first happens when you say "I do" on your wedding day. It also happens in the marriage bed—emotionally, spiritually, and physically. A neurochemical reaction of dopamine and oxytocin floods the brain to bond men and women during sex. These love hormones trigger feelings of reward and pleasure in couples, even promoting fidelity and monogamy. Becoming one flesh also describes the journey of a husband and wife traveling through life together. They carry and support each other in good times and not-so-good times. They celebrate and console. They love each other unconditionally. They give and receive. All of the above connections are designed by the One who created you, your daughter, her suitors, and marriage itself.

Some couples describe their marriage as 50/50. With that perspective, their motivation for serving each other is, "You had your turn, now it's my turn." Or, "If I do this for her, she will do something else for me." That might work for a while, but the relationship is reduced to a series of transactions. That flawed marital logic suggests if your spouse can't or won't do their part, then you owe them nothing. That's not a marriage, that's two people doing business. I think God had a better idea. As one flesh, you do something because it elevates and serves both of you. Your motivation is "If I do this for her, it brings me joy as well." That's not 50/50. That's 100/100.[1]

Men, if your relationship with your daughter's mother is strained or broken, then you need to work extra hard to make this point. Your daughter knows more than you think she knows. Using your best judgment, but making no excuses, you may want to admit your failings. You may need to ask forgiveness. Even if marriage didn't work for you, you need to talk about your daughter's future marriage with sincere optimism and hope for her future.

Insight for GirlDads: The Birds and the Bees and All That

In our local school district, most fifth-grade students get a basic lesson in how babies are made. How about your schools? That's important to know, because parents should cover this topic months before your schools present their "sex ed curriculum." You want to lay the right groundwork and make sure your daughter understands the moral and spiritual side of sexuality and procreation. Plus, by initiating the topic, she will see you as the go-to resource for any future questions—which is what you want, even though you dread them. Right?

Even if you homeschool your daughter or send her to private school, you need to know when and what the other kids in your area are learning. That's all part of knowing the culture and whether or not your values are being supported.

In general, when it comes to the physical aspects of puberty, I recommend dads talk to sons and moms talk to daughters. But for a variety of reasons, that's not always possible. If that's your situation, then begin looking now for the right aunt, grandmother, or close friend who happens to be a nurse or doctor, or a mom of one of your daughter's friends to join you or even lead this conversation. Your daughter will appreciate your sensitivity.

If you do enlist a trusted woman to engage your daughter in this area, that doesn't let you off the hook, Dad. Also, making jokes or causing her embarrassment will put up a wall that will last quite a while. See if you can find a balance between keeping your mouth shut and making yourself available as a sounding board. By handling this delicate matter with grace and respect, you will gain a bonus level of trust with your daughter that will serve you well in many future conversations—especially when it comes to boys, modesty, chastity, love, and all things related to sex and intimacy.

I believe the way parents handle "the sex talk" has a significant impact on whether young people grow up to trust God or turn their back on Him. It's that important. Consider all the issues your daughter is sorting out in this season of life: love, sex, truth, faith, womanhood, new responsibilities, changing schools, new friends, new choices for the future, and deciding whom she can trust. That time of transition for young teenagers always reminds me of 1 Corinthians 13:11: "When I was a child, I spoke and thought and reasoned as a child. But when I grew up, I put away childish things" (NLT).

By the way, "the birds-and-the-bees talk" is not a single event. It's a progressive father-daughter interaction that begins when you sing that first lullaby and continues until her wedding day.

Insight for GirlDads: Your Daughter Should Postpone Sex until Marriage

Do you agree with this insight? I think most dads do, but they're not sure how to convey that truth to their daughter. You may not even know if you have the right or responsibility. You may even be thinking, *I didn't wait, so how can I expect my own children to wait?* Plus, the culture assumes that most young people are sexually active in high school or soon thereafter. In many ways, it's an uphill battle, and you might think it's a lost cause. You're even afraid any statements made about "wearing white" at her wedding will be mocked or ignored. Well, Dad, say it anyway. Come at it from a few different angles. "Saving yourself is a gift to your future husband." "It's real easy to confuse sex with love." "On your wedding night, you will be so glad you waited." "Sweetheart, there are all kinds of reasons to wait—physical, emotional, spiritual, medical." "I hope you realize that you are worth waiting for."

Work hard on your relationship with your daughter, spending enough time with her so that you have regular opportunity to say, "You know, sex really does work best inside the sacred covenant of marriage."

Insight for GirlDads: Be Her Safe Harbor

There's a very good chance your little girl will someday have her heart broken. When that happens, say little and hug much. If the pain is fresh, tell her you love her and admit you really don't know what to say. Let her know you will always be there for her. Also, don't verbally trash the scoundrel that just broke her heart because he still someday may be your future son-in-law.

Insight for GirlDads: Killing Off the Damsel in Distress

Rae Anne was never a fragile, helpless princess. Her four older brothers made sure of that. The fact that she was an all-state catcher in high school and attended West Point underscores her mental toughness and capacity to take care of herself. Venturing off on her own to attend law school in Dublin confirms her independent spirit.

But many girls do like to take on the role of a damsel in distress. For some reason, they believe they need to present themselves as weak and defenseless to snag a boyfriend or husband. Well, guys do like to feel strong, needed, and powerful. But the smart ones—the young men worthy of your daughter—also know that somewhere down the line, they will need their wife to be strong, resourceful, and intelligent. Life happens—which means wives and husbands need to be able to unite forces to rescue each other at times. All that to say, the "damsel in distress" model your daughter may be emulating is pretty much ancient history.

Rae Anne's four older brothers found four remarkable and accomplished young ladies to wed. Lindsay, Rachel, Megan, and Kaitlin have become good friends with my daughter and excellent role models of strong, self-sufficient women. I may be a little biased, but I can confirm that each of those marriages prove that good men are attracted to strong women.

So encourage your daughter to be confident in her strengths and abilities and demonstrate her personal resourcefulness. That gives her even more freedom and confidence to let possible suitors know they are expected to be men of honor and substance.

Insight for GirlDads: Set a High Standard for Husbands

It's possible that your beautiful daughter brings home a long line of scurrilous, ill-mannered losers who are clearly unworthy of her companionship. When she introduces them—which is her absolute responsibility—those lads barely offer a weak handshake and can't even look you in the eye.

Don't be too alarmed. Because the day will come when she introduces you to a guy who just might be the one. He's confident, but not too confident. He's smart, but not a wise guy. He's athletic, but not a dumb jock. But most of all, he treats your little girl with respect and kindness. How can you increase the odds that she finds a suitor who's worthy?

It's simple, really. Be that kind of man yourself. Be the kind of husband you want your daughter to have. Be the kind of dad you want your future son-in-law to be. Make your daughter feel special. By helping your daughter realize her worth, she won't settle for any man who doesn't do the same.

If your daughter does choose marriage, don't expect your son-in-law to be your clone. But do expect him to reflect your values and your devotion to God. Expect him to love and respect your daughter even more than you do.

For years, you've been helping your daughter establish and embrace her own faith journey. Make sure you're also reinforcing the goal set forth in 2 Corinthians 6:14 that Christians should "not be yoked together with unbelievers." Otherwise, you're setting your daughter up for conflict and disunity down the road.

After walking your little girl down the aisle, you'll want to be confident that you're shaking the hand of a man who will cherish, honor, respect, and love her as a partner in life that lasts for eternity.

Insight for GirlDads: Pray for Your Daughter's Heart

Much of what dads focus on—and much of this book—is about the mindful decisions you and your daughter make over the course of life. Thinking things through. Making good choices. Building resolve that helps her reach her full potential.

However, more important than guarding her intellectual endeavors may be the idea of safeguarding her heart. Proverbs 4:23 expresses the preeminence of the heart when it comes to your daughter's well-being: "Above all else, guard your heart, for everything you do flows from it."

Your daughter's heart will assuredly face all kinds of disappointments. Friends moving away. Auditions and tryouts that don't go her way. Rejection emails from colleges and employers. But for many girls, it's romantic heartbreak that likely leaves the deepest wound.

Dad, I encourage you to pray for your daughter's heart when it comes to her boyfriends and even her future husband. Pray in private and also with her. It really shouldn't be awkward. Start early, before she even cares about boys. Make conversations and prayer about love, marriage, sex, and what to look for in a spouse a natural part of your time together.

Your male perspective can be enlightening. You don't have to warn your daughter that men can be jerks. But letting her know that young men are often wrestling with a barrel of fears, desires, and uncertainties may help her sort through her relationship woes.

Consider praying for your daughter's future husband, even though they probably haven't even met yet. Pray for God's protection on that boy who may be out there, whom God may be preparing to be a lifelong marriage partner for your little girl.

When you pray with your daughter for her future husband, you're laying the foundation for her to be a godly wife, if that's what God calls her to be. Which is an interesting point: That daughter you're praying for may be called to singleness, and that has to be okay. Take care not to put expectations on her. She doesn't have to get married.

Remember that the Apostle Paul remained single and saw it as a gift. In 1 Corinthians 7:7–8, he gives a sincere shoutout to individuals who are called to singleness:

> I wish that all of you were as I am. But each of you has your own gift from God; one has this gift, another has that. Now to the unmarried and the widows I say: It is good for them to stay unmarried, as I do.

No matter how old she is or how in love she thinks she is, your prayers should always be that your daughter hears, understands, and surrenders to God's will.

MAKE THE CHASTITY ARGUMENT

Not all at once, but over time, present to your daughter several reasons to wait until she's married to have sex, from several points of view. Feel free to use these exact words:

"You are valuable and worth waiting for." She is. Plus, she'll like hearing that from you.

"Because God says so." Absolutely true, but it's a hard sell for teenagers who may be trying to figure out their own relationship with God. "Marriage should be honored by all, and the marriage bed kept pure" (Hebrews 13:4).

"You can only give away your virginity one time." Also true. But it might not be an effective deterrent because "everyone else is doing it." To a high schooler, being a virgin seems to have lost its value and may even be a term of ridicule.

"You can't ignore the epidemic of sexually transmitted diseases." Arm yourself with just a few facts. About 25 percent of teenage girls and about 45 percent of women between the ages of twenty and twenty-four have a human papillomavirus (HPV) infection. An estimated 1.5 million new cases of chlamydia infections occur every year among fifteen- to twenty-four-year-olds, which can lead to infertility and ectopic pregnancies. HIV/AIDS is still not curable, and 56,000 new cases are diagnosed in the U.S. every year; heterosexual contact leads to more than 30 percent of the new cases.[2] Scare tactics built around STDs might work. But most teenagers see themselves as indestructible.

"I am so looking forward to the day you give me a grandchild, but here's an idea: wait until you're married." Every year in the U.S., a million unmarried women between the ages of twenty and twenty-four get pregnant. More than 500,000 become single moms. More than 400,000 abort their babies.[3]

"Dating should be about getting to know someone." The point here, of course, is that the focus of today's dating rituals is often, *When and where will we next have sex?* when it should be, *Do my boyfriend and I bring out the best in each other?*

"Waiting is a gift for your future husband." Girls like to imagine their wedding day. And maybe their wedding night. God designed sex to cement the bond between a wife and her husband. Every sexual encounter outside of marriage weakens that future bonding.

> "Sex is a gift from God to be opened at just the right time."
> This point rarely gets made when talking to teens about sex.
> There's a spiritual dimension to sexual intimacy within mar-
> riage. It's not easy to explain, but it's all part of God's design.

Rae Anne's Reality Check

I know you have imagined walking your daughter down the aisle. I know you have imagined what you would say, what you would do, how you would fight back the tears. I know you have a strong desire to see your daughter married, protected and provided for, and to see her one day present you with adorable, perfect grandchildren. I know you've had all of these thoughts in one form or another. But, as joyful and as wonderful as you may imagine that walk down the aisle to be, I want you to imagine handing her over to a man who is not worthy. Or walking her when she's not ready to be married. Or walking her when she is not truly in love. This should be your biggest nightmare.

So when you are doing all the things that my father discusses in this chapter, I want to underscore the importance of not rushing your daughter, not pushing her, and not making her feel like her worth is wrapped up in being married, that her life is incomplete or not worthwhile without a husband. Yes, marriage is a wonderful thing, and to find that one person you want to spend your entire life with is beautiful—but to enter marriage out of fear, loneliness, or pride is a dangerous path.

Fathers, please show your daughter that other life pursuits are also worthy of her time and energy, that she doesn't just have to be defined by one thing. Also, please realize that if your daughter is letting the years pass by and she is watching all her friends get married and she is not close, she knows it. She knows it more deeply and strongly than you could ever understand. Don't say things, even joking things, about her singleness. Those words would just be an echo of the thoughts in her head. Your job as a father is to love your daughter and never make her feel any less worthy for any reason, especially her relationship status.

If and when the time is right, when her heart has been prepared for the commitment of marriage—and her future husband's heart as well—everything will fall into place. On that day, you can walk down the aisle knowing that your daughter is walking toward the man and the life for which God is currently preparing her.

Hey, Rae Anne . . .

I see my teenage daughter and her friends heading towards the slippery slope of romance, and I don't know what boundaries to set.

The best way to adequately combat this inevitably slippery slope is to make these boundaries clear and understood very early. As soon as your daughter has moved into the writing notes and sharing milkshakes portion of romance, sit her down (preferably alongside her mom) and explain the guidelines and boundaries that you as her parents have set up in an attempt to best equip her for the years ahead. I encourage you to give her some room to explore these waters of romance while she is in your house and under your watch.

It is often the girls with the most restrictions who rebel the most. Don't create rules for the sake of rules.

If you have established clear standards and defined clear reasons for them before she ever starts dating, you'll head off problems before they become problems. Don't wait for the situations to arise to combat them individually. Set the rules when emotions are not running high and a civil conversation is still possible.

That being said, good boundaries to set are:

- Potential boyfriends can only be in public areas of the house.
- She cannot have him over unless one of her parents is home.
- Set curfews and wait up for her.
- Set curfews for texting and phone calls.
- Any boy who wants to take her on a date has to meet you first.

Every set of parents will have their own set of rules, but make sure she knows that the purpose behind each of them is for her safety and out of your love for her. If she thinks your rules are too strict, talk it out, answer questions, and have an open dialogue (but don't be afraid to stick to your guns).

Also, just as a side note, the rules need to be the same for your sons. While you may instinctively want to be more protective of your little girl, you are asking for a battle if you try to bind her with different rules than her older brother.

Hey, Rae Anne . . .

My daughter has dated a few boys while she has been in high school. I'm not sure what they do when they are alone, but I am worried that my daughter is making bad choices, and I don't know what to do.

Just as your daughter will go through fashion, music, and eating phases, she will have her share of romantic phases as well. She will have crushes on actors or pop stars. She will probably experience complete and total puppy love. She may date a nice, boring boy that you love because you know he wouldn't touch her with a ten-foot pole. She may date a cool and rebellious "bad boy" who makes you nervous. With one young man, she may round a few bases you would prefer she didn't, then experience a breakup, leaving her confused and hurt—not just about her physical choices, but her emotional ones too.

Now, I can almost guarantee she does not want to talk with you about this stuff, and probably does not want to talk to her mom about it, either. Still, if you are paying attention, you'll see the signs and may be able to give her some valuable guidance. Without getting into the specifics or imagery, it can be your place to tell her that she can start over. She can take a couple steps back and really consider who she wants to be and what she wants for herself.

If she did or said or felt things for one boy, that does not mean that she has to experience all those same things with the next. Remind her that in every relationship, her choices are her own, and she can learn from past mistakes in order to grow in the next relationship. She can make a new choice about her future. She really can start over. She can be whoever she wants to be, starting today. It's never too late.

Rae Anne's Reality Check

This is going to be a rough reality check for you, but it needs to be said. In this delightful little chapter, we have talked about your daughter's future marriage and even helped you imagine walking her down the aisle to begin life with some guy who is almost good enough for her. But you can't talk about boyfriends and sex without addressing the dark and unpleasant truth on the other side of that coin. Sexual assault—including difficult topics like rape and date rape—is a reality in today's world. While it has always existed, in the past few years, we have seen the toll it has taken on our college campuses and even in our high schools. Current research confirms that one in five women will be sexually assaulted by the time they leave college. Picture your daughter with her starting basketball squad. Picture her with her four best friends from kindergarten. Chances are one of those girls will be sexually assaulted. *One in five.*[4]

As a witness to some of the aftermath of this crisis, I have plenty of choice words to say to the collegiate men and the fathers of men who propel this culture. But right now, I am talking to you, the father of a little girl who has a 20 percent chance of being marked as a victim. She needs to be warned. You cannot allow her to walk into the world without knowing the truth about the destructive mindset of so many young men, the dangers that lie beyond the threshold of fraternity doors, the terrifying nature of roofies, and the concept of date rape. Equip her with self-preservation skills that unfortunately include not trusting some boys who seem trustworthy. You raised her to be an optimist and to see the best in people. Well, you need to add some healthy suspicion to her perspective on men.

When it comes to the big picture, fathers like you should take every chance to teach the young men in your life about the importance of consent and how it is very much up to the male populace to end this horrible problem. Even as you protect your own daughter, accept that this problem doesn't end with your family. Every girl that makes up that 20 percent was once a three-year-old princess like yours, was once a nervous six-year-old at her first day of school, is someone's daughter, and is an individual with value, potential, hopes, and dreams. They deserve better. This very real and urgent problem affects all of us, and when you look at your little girl, you should get angry and you should get loud about it.

"You fathers will understand. You have a little girl. An adorable little girl who looks up to you and adores you in a way you could never have imagined. I remember how her little hand used to fit inside mine. Then comes the day when she wants to get her ears pierced and wants you to drop her off a block before the movie theater. From that moment on you're in a constant panic. You worry about her meeting the wrong kind of guy, the kind of guy who only wants one thing, and you know exactly what that one thing is, because it's the same thing you wanted when you were their age. Then, you stop worrying about her meeting the wrong guy, and you worry about her meeting the right guy. That's the greatest fear of all, because then you lose her."

—Steve Martin as George Banks, *Father of the Bride*

CHAPTER EIGHT

Your Daughter and Her Self-Image

*We can never know who or what we are till we know
at least something of what God is.*

—A. W. Tozer

Let's start with this idea. Dad, you have no idea what it's like to be a girl in today's culture. Even the most confident, brilliant, and beautiful young lady goes through long seasons when she feels the exact opposite of confident, brilliant, and beautiful.

But it gets worse. Adolescent girls receive an onslaught of mixed messages regarding who they should become, what they should want, and how to maneuver through life. Even smart girls are misinformed and susceptible to irrational behavior. Plus, they get acne, wear braces, have weird growth spurts, and are still experimenting with makeup, hairstyles, and their wardrobe.

Which means your pre-teen or teenage daughter is *not* confident, brilliant, or beautiful. In your heart, you may totally see her as confident, brilliant, and beautiful. But the world does not see her that way. And she certainly doesn't.

Here's where it gets a little tricky. Only one person on Earth has the right, privilege, and responsibility to look at your daughter and truthfully say, "You are so beautiful." "You can do anything." "You are so clever." "You have so much to offer." "You're the best." Dad, that person is you.

Your goal—and the reason this book exists—is for you to build a relationship with your daughter and earn the right to say those things. And make sure that she believes you when you do.

When most girls look in the mirror, they don't like what they see. When they page through a fashion magazine, they know they don't measure up. When a boy offers a compliment, they know he may be just delivering a line. Girls crave approval from their friends, but still question the sincerity of any flattery or praise. Even affirmation from your daughter's mother rings insincere. A girl knows that Mom will say anything sometimes just to get her out the door without changing her clothes again or tying up the bathroom for another twenty minutes.

No pressure, Dad. But your words and your attitude have a significant, lifelong impact on your daughter's self-image, self-esteem, and self-confidence.

Insight for GirlDads: Speak into Her Life

Conventional wisdom suggests that women speak three times as many words as men over the course of a day. If that's anywhere close to true, it suggests that well-chosen words are important to the women in your life—including your daughter at every age and stage.

So here's a gift for dads, especially those who are not particularly verbal. Deliver the following short phrases as part of your regular routine. Whisper them at bedtime. Text them. Say them casually without looking up from your tablet as your daughter enters a room. Shout them as she heads out the door. Jot them on yellow Post-It notes and leave them on her book bag, purse, bedroom door, violin case, alarm clock, mirror, or steering wheel.

"Have a great day, sweetie." "So proud of you." "See you at the concert tonight." "XOXO." "Missed you yesterday." "Really sorry about our tiff last night. Love, Dad." "Tennis this weekend?" "Thanks for emptying the DW last nite!" "Praying for you." "Need your advice on mom's BD gift." "Hope today goes better." "Good luck at tryouts. Love, your biggest fan." "Text me when you get there." "Love ya."

Are you cringing at some of these short phrases? That's okay. Several of them could make your daughter cringe as well. But they do express sentiments and truths she needs to hear. Words of gratitude. Words of hope. Words that can only come from you. Frankly, Dad, I think you should go out on a limb and try a few of them out in the next few days. You want to, I know. Ask yourself what's the worst that could happen. You may get an eyeroll. You may get a verbal response such as, "Dad! Where did that come from?" But—even if it comes off like you're trying too hard—your little girl will know that you're, well, trying. You're thinking about her. You're on her side, cheering for her. To a young woman who's trying to find her place in this frantic, judgmental world, having a dad who's trying too hard is actually a warm fuzzy that shouldn't be dismissed.

Communication within families is taking a hit these days. Without being intentional, a dad and daughter could go a full week without any significant connection. Your brief encouraging words—scribbled in a note or even just spoken in passing—may be exactly what she needs to hear this very day. An optimistic nudge from you may be the only thing countering the dark forces of the world telling her stuff that drags her down and makes her feel unworthy and unloved.

Insight for GirlDads: Don't Give Conditional Compliments

You love your daughter unconditionally. But sometimes your compliments seem to come with some conditional baggage. You say something nice, but follow up with a slam or criticism.

"Hey, sweetie. The lawn looks great. Did you sweep the grass off the sidewalk?"

"This beautiful drawing is for me?! That's fantastic. But I thought you were supposed to be cleaning your room."

"Your coach said your footwork has really improved. Now you just need to start getting your first serve in."

"Thanks for watching the baby. But you left the lid off the diaper pail."

Now go back and reread those same four statements, but leave off the final sentence. Making conditional compliments is like driving the green and then four-putting. Nice start, but total fail.

I do get it. As dads, we're trying to point out areas in which your daughter can improve or how little things make a difference. But, once in a while, we should deliver an uplifting message without any lesson attached. You can do that, right?

Insight for GirlDads: Almost All Girls Think They're Fat

Anorexia and bulimia are real. An article in the *Journal of Pediatric Psychology* reports that 35 to 57 percent of adolescent girls engage in crash dieting, fasting, self-induced vomiting, or use diet pills or laxatives.[1] According to one state mental health department, women are seven times more likely to have an eating disorder than men.[2] Among the most disturbing statistics I ran across on the topic of body image is this: 42 percent of first- through third-grade girls want to be thinner.[3]

Yikes. What's going on and how should a caring father respond? Well, don't pretend eating disorders are just a phase. It's actually a life-or-death situation. Anorexia nervosa has the highest mortality rate of any psychiatric disorder.[4] If you have any immediate concerns, please get better informed—pursuing information beyond anything you read in this chapter—and get professional help.

I believe much of the problem is that the entire world is telling your daughter she cannot be happy unless she loses some weight. Again, that's true for girls of all shapes and sizes.

As her daddy, you would never intentionally be part of any evil attack on your daughter's self-regard. Well-meaning dads say things they believe are harmless or even helpful. But the words they use *do* harm and they *don't* help. Examples: "Are you getting enough exercise?" "Why don't you eat an apple instead?" "It's funny how your sister can eat so much and doesn't put on any weight." "Did you know there are 140 calories in a can of Coke?" "My Aunt Ruth was overweight."

To your ears, none of these may sound like an attack. But if they come out of your mouth, your lovely, sweet, and trusting little girl is going to hear this: "Daughter, you're fat." If that sounds harsh, that's because it is harsh. Very harsh. If you don't believe me, ask your wife.

Insight for GirlDads: Expect Her Temporary Retreat

At a surprisingly young age, most girls already have experienced significant bruising in key relationships—abandoned by a best friend, teased by a classmate, or hurt by someone she trusted.

Maybe she's feeling disconnected from her brother or sister simply because of a brief disagreement or moment of jealousy. Maybe she's actually disappointed in herself. She said something she regrets. She knows she could be doing better at school. She set some personal goals that were a bit too ambitious. Or maybe it's something you said or did, Dad, that has caused her to shrink from the world.

You can't blame her for setting up boundaries and building protective walls. She may still have a dollhouse collecting dust in the corner of her room, but most of her time is spent creating places and spaces off-limits to parents. Especially dads. Her safe space includes physical locations like her bedroom. But it also includes a kind of forbidden zone she creates with the aura she puts out. Sitting in a chair or just walking in a room, she can make it clear that she does not want to be disturbed. Add some electronics in her hands or ears, and she's unreachable.

How do you handle this retreat from the family? Should you agonize or mourn the season when she stops sitting on your lap?

First, don't assume you've done something wrong. Also, don't assume it's permanent. My advice is don't overreact. Look for moments when she does smile and then simply smile back. If she opens her door a bit, make her glad she did. Some dads might think, *Fine, if you don't want to hang out with me, I'll find something I'd rather be doing.* But like all women, your daughter wants to be pursued. Even wooed. So keep entering her space and asking her on mini-dates. When she says, "Sure, Dad," go ahead and make a little bit of a big deal about it. But not too big.

Soon enough, your relationship will come full circle and your daughter will regularly want your full attention, wisdom, and level-headed advice regarding many of the weighty and trivial issues facing teenage girls today. Don't miss that moment. Make sure you're available because—as always—she'll be counting on her dad.

Insight for GirlDads: Help Her See Her True Value

Your daughter doesn't know how wonderful she is. As stated above, your words have the power to make her feel a little more confident, a little more cherished. But even a well-spoken father delivering all the wisdom of the world cannot convey the true value of a girl, her life, and her very soul.

You see, the true value of a person has no price tag. The true value of your daughter cannot be found on this planet. She is worth far more than all the gold, diamonds, and rubies in the world. Clearly stated, your daughter is worth Jesus.

If that idea comes as a surprise, allow me to explain. To describe what Jesus did on the cross, theologians sometimes use the phrase "substitutionary atonement." Those two words summarize the heart of the Gospel: We've all sinned, and the punishment for those sins is our responsibility, but with His death on the cross, Jesus paid that price for each of us as individuals. Including your daughter.

Three passages from the Bible make it clear.

> Surely he took up our pain and bore our suffering, yet we considered him punished by God, stricken by him, and afflicted. But he was pierced for our transgressions, he was crushed for our iniquities; the punishment that brought us peace was on him, and by his wounds we are healed. (Isaiah 53:4–5)

God made him who had no sin to be sin for us, so that
in him we might become the righteousness of God.
(2 Corinthians 5:21)

"He himself bore our sins" in his body on the cross, so
that we might die to sins and live for righteousness; "by
his wounds you have been healed." (1 Peter 2:24)

This is critical for your daughter to understand. Jesus loved us
so much that He took on the separation from God and eternal death
that we deserve. Another term painting a picture of what happened
on the cross is "The Great Exchange." For each of us as individuals,
our inferior self is replaced by a new righteousness. The "old me"
was nailed up on that cross and exchanged for a "new person."

Perhaps your most important job as her father is to help your
daughter understand and accept that free gift of grace. To see that
she is worth Jesus. For her to look in the mirror and see the resur-
rected Christ—beautiful and worthy.

Insight for GirlDads: Help Her Find Greatness

I pretty much hate the term "self-esteem" because of the many
middle school courses that propose to teach kids that everything
they think or do is the most wonderful thing ever thought or done.
In those silly classes with the silly names, young teens are taught to
"be true to yourself." And to "search your heart and just do what
you think is best."

How does that sound to you? Do you want to live in a world
in which teens follow their own undisciplined whims and wishes?

That would be chaos. Young people need to know that absolute truth exists beyond their own opinions, their own desires, and their own little world. They need to know there is a moral certainty.

Self-esteem cannot come from within. But self-esteem can come from putting God first. Scripture is filled with confirmation that life is not about finding yourself. It's about finding God's plan for your life, identifying your gifts, and committing to use those gifts to give glory back to Him.

> Commit to the Lord whatever you do, and he will establish your plans. (Proverbs 16:3)

> Seek first his kingdom and his righteousness, and all these things will be given to you as well. (Matthew 6:33)

> Jesus said to his disciples, "Whoever wants to be my disciple must deny themselves and take up their cross and follow me. For whoever wants to save their life will lose it, but whoever loses their life for me will find it." (Matthew 16:24–25)

Earlier chapters—about your daughter's hopes and dreams, extracurricular activities, and relationships—laid the groundwork for this all-important revelation. It's not about her. It's not about you. Greatness comes when we realize that "He must increase, but I must decrease" (John 3:30 NASB). That's how and when a young girl will appropriately feel confident, brilliant, and beautiful.

Rae Anne's Reality Check

Just as I made my father write the chapter on brokenness, he insisted on including this chapter concerning self-image over my initial concerns. Originally, it was going to focus solely on body image, and we compromised to include the idea that self-image is also tied to self-confidence, finding your purpose, and seeing your value as a follower of Christ.

My inclination to avoid the topic of self-image was in no way because I believe that body image is not a crucial part of a young woman's identity, quite the contrary. I simply did not believe that there is anything a father can do. But as I quarreled with my own dad about this chapter, I realized there are things a father *shouldn't* do, which are maybe just as important. You, as her father, have more influence in this area than you can possibly understand. She will take your every word and every tone and store them away in her heart and mind. Your amazing power can be used for destruction or empowerment.

You know how a romantic partner will take an innocent or inadvertent word as an insult, leaving you in the proverbial doghouse? Increase that impact exponentially, and you will barely begin to understand the weight of your words in your young daughter's ears. Evaluate everything you say before you say it. It does not matter what you intended to say; it only matters how it is received.

There are so many voices speaking hateful and judgmental words into your daughter's life, including the media, her classmates, and most powerfully, her own inner voice. She knows every one of her flaws, ones you cannot even begin to guess. What she desperately needs you to be is silent on the matter. Silent—not positive. If your daughter is not beautiful, she knows she is not beautiful, so don't lie to her. If your daughter is not smart, she knows she is not smart, so don't lie to her. Instead speak truths. Compliment her actual traits, make her feel strong in the things she is good at and the strengths she has. Physical beauty is only one aspect of a woman. It is your job to give things like intelligence, kindness, humor, faith, and honesty equal footing in her mind. You cannot empower her with falsehoods that she knows are lies. But you can empower her with honest compliments that instill confidence in her whole sense of self.

Hey, Rae Anne . . .

My daughter wants expensive things. Clothes, jewelry, handbags. Most of it I don't understand. Should I buy her these things? Am I teaching her a bad lesson if I do?

This is a common affliction among preteen and teenage girls, and you are certainly not the first father to hold shopping bags as his wife and daughter make their way through the mall. But what it comes down to is this: what is your daughter's motivation for wanting these things?

I see three possible scenarios: 1) She has an authentic high-end taste for things and genuinely wants these products. 2) She has thought through the cost-benefit analysis and knows that more expensive things will last longer and thus are a good investment. Or 3) She is trying to impress someone, probably the other girls her age. Chances are, it's the last.

So have that conversation. When I was in middle school, literally 95 percent of the girls would wear the same $150 jeans with holes in the knees and the same four tops from Hollister and American Eagle—and I still genuinely believe the only reason was because everyone else was wearing it. The same goes with purses, phones, earrings, etc. When your daughter asks you for something, ask her why she wants it. If she replies with anything that insinuates it's to impress someone else, ask her why that's so important. Use this opportunity to show her that her value is not in her possessions or how much money she can spend, but in her character. Maybe give her a somewhat low limit on her fashion budget, and have her see how she could buy one expensive thing or several less expensive, yet just as attractive, items. Maybe she needs to get a part-time job if she wants to buy high-end products; then she will attribute each purchase with the hours of labor she has put into earning the money.

If all she cares about is the price tag, there is a fundamental problem in how she views value, and most likely, how she views the value of the people around her. You'll need to address that directly.

Rae Anne's Reality Check

Your daughter was born with a set of natural God-given attributes, talents, skills, and qualities—things that come naturally to her, such as eloquence, athleticism, beauty, humor, etc. Some girls are granted more natural gifts than others, but when all is said and done, the only way your daughter will truly succeed is if she works hard to achieve something on her own, actually putting those gifts to work. You know this. This is not anything that you haven't fought through yourself.

So I encourage you to place value not just in your daughter's attributes, but in the way she tries, the way she works, and the desire in her heart. Compliment her on the sweat she pours over a task, whether she fails or succeeds. Her value is not just in the qualities she has, but in what she does with them. Her value is not only in nouns like beauty and intelligence, but in verbs like trying, fighting, learning, and struggling. Help her to understand the value of hard work, determination, and setting, seeking, and achieving a goal. That's how she will see herself grow and take ownership and pride in not only who she is, but what she does.

Hey, Rae Anne . . .

My middle school-aged daughter has become obsessed with beauty regimes, makeup, and celebrity styles. I'm worried that she is becoming too wrapped up in superficial things.

While the things you have listed are not evil in nature, as with all worldly things, when they become the center of your life, dangers follow. There is a chance this phase will be over very soon. As young girls discover the arena of makeup and fashion, sometimes they get swept up in the novelty of it all. You should also expect an obsession with celebrities followed by a fascination with fame and fortune—all of which is a natural outlet for girls' curiosity and daydreaming as they approach adulthood. Oftentimes, your daughter is just looking at the different ways people express themselves in order to figure out how she wants to express herself in the future. It's a fun discovery process. But you can use this phase and "obsession" to gauge and guide your daughter's understanding of what is valuable in life.

If she is drawn to an actress, ask her why. Is it because of her talent and skill on the screen, or her popularity with the kids your daughter's age? Why does she idolize one woman over another? Show her the effect of photoshop on the pictures in magazines that she may try to emulate. Explain how the world is trying to impose expectations that are impossible to reach. Ask her whether she would rather spend time with a beautiful person or a kind person. Would she rather be seen as stylish or loving? Do not demonize her new fixation, but use this phase to help her examine her priorities. Ask a lot of why questions and suggest a lot of hypothetical scenarios.

Here's the hard part: Don't lecture. Let her sort out the truth for herself. As with most things, the solution begins with an honest conversation with your daughter, and an attempt to understand her and help her understand herself.

"Your beauty should not come from outward adornment, such as elaborate hairstyles and the wearing of gold jewelry or fine clothes. Rather, it should be that of your inner self, the unfading beauty of a gentle and quiet spirit, which is of great worth in God's sight."

—1 Peter 3:3–4

"Look in a mirror and one thing is sure; what we see is not who we are."

—Richard Bach

CHAPTER NINE

Your Daughter and Her Time with You

No one in this world can love a girl more than her father.

—Michael Ratnadeepak

Some dads find it easier to relate to boys. With sons, they rough-house a little more. They are more likely to play a game of catch. A man's own hobbies and interests often seem to match his son's hobbies and interests.

So as the dad of a daughter, you need to stay aware of that tendency and be intentional about making time for just you and her.

It's really okay that boys and girls are different. Girls relate. Boys explore. Girls are more verbal. Boys are more physical. Little girls really do hold tea parties and play with dolls. Little boys really are fascinated by trucks and will pretend to shoot things from any stick shaped like a gun. You don't want to put any of your kids in a box, and there probably is some cultural bias going on, but it is what it is.

Don't feel guilty. Don't try to overcorrect or change the natural order. You don't have to buy your daughter a shotgun and football helmet—but you do need to understand who she is and what makes her tick, which means spending focused time with just her. Sometimes that's doing her stuff. Sometimes that's inviting her to join in your stuff. Even better, it could be creatively trying out a bunch of different activities until one feels right for the two of you to do together for whatever season of life you're in right now.

You've heard it before, and maybe you've experienced it: Kids grow so quickly. You can't stop it, but you can capture moments. That's going to require you to be intentional, Dad. Can you do that?

Insight for GirlDads: Making Time Now

I don't know how many kids you have. Maybe it's just you and your daughter. But if you have a family of three, four, or more, you'll want to spend lots of time doing lots of stuff making lots of memories. That includes backyard shenanigans, dinner-table debates, bedtime rituals, camping adventures, beach frolicking, city exploring, and trips to Grandma's house.

Based on my experience with our five kids, you can pretty much count on those big family memories all blurring together. That's not a bad thing. As a family, we've been left with the overwhelming impression that there was never a dull moment, and I miss those days.

But between the big family extravaganzas, your daughter needs breakthrough moments of just you and her. Whether she says it or not, she craves time alone with Dad to make her feel special and cherished. That doesn't happen without some intentional decisions on your part.

The greatest truth about time with your daughter is this: If you make time for her when she's little, she'll make time for you later. The good news is that finding time with a preschooler is easy. Ten minutes here or there blowing bubbles, chasing butterflies, or making valentines for Mom will forge those critical connections and establish a lifelong pattern.

By school age, time with your daughter should probably expand, but it's still not complicated. Think of each room in your home as having its own appeal: play a board game in the dining room, share a chapter book in her bedroom, make salsa in the kitchen, play ping-pong in the basement, and do hopscotch on the front sidewalk. Leave the house to walk in the woods, share a banana split, browse the library, or shop for something to enhance her current sport or hobby. You could even stop and pet puppies at the local kennel. (Just don't take one home without asking Mom.)

Insight for GirlDads: Engaging a Teen's Attention

When your daughter begins her transition from daddy's little girl to busy-can't-be-disturbed teenager, you will need a few strategies allowing you to interrupt her jam-packed schedule and get her to put down her phone.

One strategy for engagement is to give her a taste of adulthood. Teens appreciate that glimpse of their future. Ask her opinion regarding a major purchase you're planning. Trust her with a responsibility that challenges her in a new way. Invite her to join a grown-up conversation about current events.

Another strategy is to take that idea a step further and treat her like an expert. Practically, that makes a lot of sense. Quite literally, she knows things you might not. For example, she knows smartphone tricks you could probably use, so ask her to recommend an app for one of your ongoing life frustrations. She also knows more about fashion than you, which is both helpful and dreadful. If she's getting high marks in language arts at school, ask her to proofread that sales sheet or website you're working on. If she's developing her graphic design skills, have her look over a layout, window display, or design project. If she's a big sister, ask her advice on how to motivate or discipline her younger brother or sister.

Think of it this way: Start treating her like a responsible adult, and she may start acting like one.

Perhaps the easiest way to get her attention is to ask her opinion or perspective on something that matters to her. That may include school schedules, reality TV, the Marvel Comics universe, worship songs, dog breeds, boy bands, pizza toppings, or the speed trap on Park Street.

Once your teenage daughter realizes that it's not always painful to engage in conversation with her dad, then you can shrewdly transition to topics that have piqued your own curiosity. That, of course, may include your daughter's unspoken plans for this weekend, this summer, and after graduation, as well as all those other things she may not be spilling her guts about. Of course, advanced interrogation techniques are not recommended.

Insight for GirlDads: Take Advantage of That Local Daddy-Daughter Dance

Each year, park districts, schools, community centers, country clubs, and even churches around the country schedule something called the "Daddy-Daughter Dance."

For the uninitiated, here's what you can expect: The events are just dads (and maybe some granddads or uncles) and their daughters up to about fifth grade. No moms or brothers allowed. The dads wear anything from nice shirts and slacks to tuxedos. The young ladies are dressed in their finest party dresses, hair done just so, and all the jewelry they might own. When she was about five, Rae Anne insisted on wearing a princess tiara she had somehow acquired, and that was just fine with me. After raising four court jesters, she was indeed my princess.

You can be as formal and chivalrous as you want, but do consider ringing your own doorbell, pinning on a corsage, posing for pictures, helping your daughter with her coat, opening car doors, and just generally being gallant. The event probably does not include dinner but will have snacks and beverages. Bonus activities may include a magician or clown, balloon animals, complimentary photos, and party favors.

The highlight of the event is the dance itself—ninety minutes of songs you know and love that will have you and your daughter(s) singing along and shaking your booties. Every town seems to have a DJ that specializes in daddy-daughter events, and that person knows how to get the crowd moving. The younger girls playfully swing on their daddy's arms or race around the floor. But the older girls—not quite young women—have a certain unspoken wistfulness about them as they know that childhood is coming to an end. The dads know that, too. Often, this will be the last time they dance together until her wedding reception more than a decade away.

A word of warning: You will want to mentally prepare yourself to surrender to the instructions of the DJ. Even if you're not a dancing kind of guy, getting out on the floor is an essential part of the evening. If you are instructed to put your right foot in and shake it all about, just do it. If a human locomotive chugs by, grab on. And please don't forget how to spell Y-M-C-A.

The evening will go by quickly. So will the years. Pretty soon, your daughter will be in middle school, way too mature for the organized "Daddy-Daughter Dance." When that happens, you will want to make sure you schedule your own scaled-down version of the event for just you and her. As described in the Insight above, your date may not include any dancing, but your conversation by candlelight may include some unexpected new information about what's going on in her life. You may even talk about boys, ambitions, and silly stuff that brothers and moms just don't get.[1]

Insight for GirlDads: Have "Our" Stuff

Not all at once, but over the course of the next couple years, see if you can identify a few places, events, or things that become connecting points for you and your little girl. Things like, "Our movie." "Our song." "Our restaurant." "Our book (or book series.)" "Our video game." "Our secret signal that says *I love you*." "Our park bench." "Our annual weekend." "Our booth at McDonald's." "Our emoji." "Our podcast." "Our scripture verse."

How do you begin to identify a restaurant or park bench as "ours"? Well, you want to make it seem organic and spontaneous. Something that just "happens." But there are ways you can help orchestrate that.

For example, invite your young daughter for breakfast at McDonald's. Choose an open booth. A few weeks later, go again and sit in the same booth. Then do it again. Eventually the two of you will be walking away from the cash register with your tray of food and someone will be sitting in your regular spot. In that moment, your booth becomes *your booth*. You can even whisper to your daughter, "Oh my goodness! Those scoundrels are sitting in our booth. Should I alert the manager?"

The same approach applies to that certain park bench, restaurant, or even an emoji. It comes down to repetition. If you sign off on a text to your daughter with a silly, unique emoji a few times in a row, that little piece of art could be an unspoken connection that brings smiles to both the sender and receiver for as long as smartphones exist.

Some mutual connecting points should be spoken right out loud. You can certainly imagine yourself saying, "Hey, Clara. We haven't been to our restaurant in a while." Or, "There's our bench! Let's sit for a bit."

Especially when Mom and any siblings are gone for the evening, you should take advantage of that chance to do something that's "just yours." Go out for sushi. Order pizza with anchovies. Make four-alarm chili. Watch old Harry Potter movies. Listen to Motown classics. Play Settlers of Catan. It comes down to identifying preferences and creating shared experiences. Rae Anne and I could watch *You've Got Mail* once a week for the next decade and it would still be engaging.

As for "our Scripture verse," go ahead and pick one. Sign it in a note to your daughter this week and then again on her next birthday card. If you happen to see it on a plaque or wall hanging, take it home as a just-because gift. For sure, you can find some version of it on Pinterest. Inscribe it on a ring or bracelet charm. Find a verse that has personal meaning for the two of you. You may want to consider, "I thank my God every time I remember you"

(Philippians 1:3) or "Seek first his kingdom and his righteousness, and all these things will be given to you as well" (Matthew 6:33). You might even develop a shorthand version of those verses that you can whisper or chirp anytime your daughter heads out the door, like "Every time" or "Seek first."

Insight for GirlDads: Where Does She Turn?

Ask yourself where your daughter goes for advice. It's really okay if you sometimes feel out of the loop. You want her to have several streams for good advice and wisdom. The Bible teaches, "Plans fail for lack of counsel, but with many advisers they succeed" (Proverbs 15:22).

Good friends can provide her with much-needed intel regarding her daily concerns about teachers, coaches, cultural movements, current events, and boys who are bad news. Youth pastors should offer discernment when it comes to the trends threatening today's young people. As we've said, her mom should be able to provide all kinds of welcome insight—sometimes as a friend, sometimes as an adversary. Even your daughter's male friends can be a valuable resource as she learns to navigate the treacherous world of human relationships.

But Dad, your advice and wisdom may carry more weight than anyone else's. When she was six, you knew everything. She hung on your every word, and you rarely steered her wrong. As she presses into her tween and teen years, you need to double down on building her trust. The challenge is that sometimes you don't know the right thing to do or say. Many of the questions she has don't have easy answers. And hear me now, it's okay to admit that. As a matter of fact, a little humility and uncertainty on your part will bring the two of you closer together.

Films and fiction are filled with authoritative fathers who drive their daughters away because they refuse to listen, have their minds made up, and rule with an iron fist. The authoritarian father may be a cliché, but the warning is valid. Dad, you do have many answers your daughter needs, but you don't have all of them. What's more, you can't possibly expect her to respect your admonitions if she feels like she's not being heard. That's how bedroom doors get slammed in your face.

Your best strategy when your daughter comes to you with a problem is to follow the advice of James 1:19–20: "Take note of this: Everyone should be quick to listen, slow to speak and slow to become angry, because human anger does not produce the righteousness that God desires."

It really does come back to hearing her heart. Even if you enter a conversation with full knowledge of the best godly advice, the very act of internalizing what she's saying will help you frame your recommendations and expectations in a way that your daughter will find copacetic.

By the way, the art of listening is more than just hearing words. It's about seeing her side of any request or story. It also requires you to ask nonjudgmental, clarifying questions. In the end of any engagement—especially the challenging ones—you'll want to feel like you're on the same side. Because you are!

Insight for GirlDads: Dating Your Daughter

This chapter—and an ongoing theme of this entire book—has been about the rewards of spending both quantity and quality time with your little girl. From age to age and season to season.

If I haven't made it clear, let me emphasize this is not a burden to bear. It's a blessing. Daddy-daughter time is a gift from a generous God who knows the importance of human relationships. If it's been a while since you spent one-on-one time with your daughter, don't feel overwhelmed with guilt. Instead, surrender to the feeling that there are experiences and insights you've been missing. Moments of connection. Shared emotions. Laughter and silliness. Hopes and dreams. Fears and frustrations. Respect and appreciation. Hugs and snuggles.

For sure, part of dating your daughter is modeling for her how she should expect to be treated by any boy who takes her out, courts her, or dares to ask for her hand in marriage.

But it's even more than that. The intentional time spent with your daughter is when you fulfill your responsibility to teach her the two most important fundamental skills for life: how to love, and how to be loved.

Rae Anne's Reality Check

I think I need to clear something up for the record. The tiara that my father speaks of in this chapter was a cheap plastic toy that my mother had recently given me for my sixth birthday and obviously, it was the exact right accessory for a Daddy-Daughter Dance. So please, to my friends that may be reading, cut me a bit of slack when you choose to mock me for my princess-dressing ways. The phase lasted roughly ninety days. That being said, I don't think anyone would accuse me of being a proverbial "girly-girl." At a young age, I replaced tiaras with baseball hats and opted out of ballet for soccer. But I do confess I did enjoy the ninety-day tiara phase. (I went through a heck of a lot of other phases as well.)

In the same way, your princess, tomboy, or superhero will naturally go through phases of fashion, music, trends, friendships, and everything in between. So when you try to enter her world or combat her temporary retreat, expect constant changes. When your competitive, aggressive, athletic six-year-old wants to wear a tiara, tell her it looks perfect. When your student council-running and academic-focused sixteen-year-old wants to take taekwondo, set up a punching bag in the basement. Be excited when your daughter chooses new things and searches for new horizons, because at the very least, it will be a ninety-day phase you can laugh about in twenty years. It's also entirely possible that she could find something that makes her happy and gives her purpose for decades to come. Partner with her in her pursuits because you don't want to be left behind when she finds whatever it is she is looking for.

Hey, Rae Anne . . .

I can't have a conversation with my daughter. I just don't ever know what to say. I don't even know where to start.

This is not as uncommon as you may think. As your daughter grows older and becomes more independent, gaining friends and experiences that you are not intricately involved with, you will feel yourself drifting from her until suddenly you are watching her life from the outside looking in. This is the natural course. As your daughter starts to spend more time without you, as she enters school and is old enough to travel to and from places alone, she will naturally grow apart from you. Conversations will be difficult, and understanding her perspective will become a bit more challenging. If you struggle to have intimate conversations in general or relate to your daughter in any capacity, the best advice I can give you is to start slow and small.

When I was seven, my father and I saw the preview for a new TV show called *Ed*, about a bowling alley-owning lawyer, and we decided we would watch it together. Now, of course this was before the era of DVRs or Netflix, so once a week at the same time we would have a designated hour together. Because of the nature of the show, we would also have a designated topic for discussion. In the current era of television on demand, you can easily find a show about a common interest and find a time slot that works for the pair of you. We got lucky in that the ongoing themes and topics surrounding *Ed* were not too controversial. If you pick a show, you'll want to take your daughter's age and maturity into consideration.

If literature is more of a common ground, read a book together. The point is to find something the two of you can do together and commit to it. Really it could be anything from history, entertainment, pop culture, or some weird hobby in which your daughter shows some interest. The doors for conversations will open and then build from there. Start to get to know your daughter again, like you did when she was three. That TV show—and the time spent with my dad—were important to me. Your show may be ridiculous and get canceled after half a season. In that case, it will be something the two of you can laugh about ten years later, but the time and effort put into that one-on-one shared experience will stand the test of time.

Hey, Rae Anne . . .

I have two daughters, and I have a lot more in common and just enjoy spending time with one more than the other. Should I feel guilty?

"Guilty" is an interesting term. I would say that you should not feel guilty about having more in common with and wanting to spend more time with one daughter over another. You are not the first parent to have a favorite child, and you certainly will not be the last. Where your "guilt" should come in is if you act on your favoritism, neglecting one daughter in favor of the other. If that's the case, I'm guessing your non-favorite daughter knows how you feel. If anything, you need to overcompensate with the effort you put into the relationship with the second daughter. If it's simply a matter of having nothing in common, find something, anything to relate to. If all else fails, choose one of her favorite things and let her teach you and intentionally make it a favorite thing of yours. That will be time well spent. She needs to know you love her, and you need to reaffirm that in yourself.

It's worth repeating. Be very careful in your relationship with your favorite to not spurn the other. Never, and I mean never, allow yourself to be a member of a two-versus-one mentality against your second. Both girls probably know how you feel. They can sense the favoritism, so it's your job as the father to combat that. In general, it's also a very smart bet to never, even in a joking matter, say the words "You're my favorite" or "She's my favorite." Your daughters are two people on two different spectrums, so do not compare them because they are incomparable. The world will naturally compare siblings and their achievements; your children do not need that from you as well.

Rae Anne's Reality Check

You may not know this now, but you want your daughter to surpass you. You want her to do things you never imagined and learn things you never knew. You want her to achieve greatness because, in a very real way, her achievements are your achievements. Keep this in mind for that day in the not-too-distant future when you ask for her help or when you turn to her for knowledge you don't have.

When that happens, consider it a good day and a victory for fathers everywhere. When your little girl, to whom you once explained the concept of iodine when she asked you what that brown bottle of burning stuff was that you put on her scraped knees, explains to you what your blood tests mean because she's halfway through medical school. When the little girl, whom you taught about the three branches of government, explains the geopolitical and social causes of the Vietnam War and how that affects the economic climate in Asia today. When the little girl who you taught to throw a softball explains to you the strategies of different bunt coverages or the intricacies of first-and-third situations that you never knew. When this day comes that she surpasses you, when you don't know something, or when you have to ask a question, do not feel stupid or inadequate or allow your pride to be hurt. Instead, bask in the joy that your daughter climbed new heights and conquered new arenas outside the realm you gave her. You have successfully equipped her for the life she chose to lead. (And chances are, you still know a few more things than her.)

The point is—on this good day—your relationship will change to a relationship of peers as opposed to that of mentor and padawan. It's an exciting time. The conversations no longer have to be stunted or muted; they can be passionate discussions between intellectual equals. This is the time when you and your daughter can become friends. So embrace your daughter's growth. She may have something to teach, and you will have entered the golden years of time spent with each other.

"It is admirable for a man to take his son fishing, but there is a special place in heaven for the father who takes his daughter shopping."

—John Sinor

"The father of a daughter is nothing but a high-class hostage. A father turns a stony face to his sons, berates them, shakes his antlers, paws the ground, snorts, runs them off into the under-brush, but when his daughter puts her arm over his shoulder and says, 'Daddy, I need to ask you something,' he is a pat of butter in a hot frying pan."

—Garrison Keillor

CHAPTER TEN

Your Daughter and Her Dad

Certain is it that there is no kind of affection so purely angelic as of a father to a daughter. In love to our wives there is desire; to our sons, ambition; but to our daughters there is something which there are no words to express.

—*Joseph Addison*

This last chapter turns the tables a bit. Once again, I'm going to give Rae Anne the credit for what you're about to read for two reasons. First, this chapter topic was her idea. Second, she's right.

Here's the overarching point: Being a girl dad made me a better person, and it can do the same for you.

Knowing Rae Anne has made me think deeper, work harder, laugh heartier, and love more. But the more universal benefit of being a girl dad is this: The time you invest in getting to know your daughter's strengths will help you better understand the differences between men and women.

For sure, the last two generations have seen many of the cultural, political, and economic disparities diminish. That undeniable revolution will likely give your daughter opportunities that were previously unthinkable. But gender differences have been the norm from the beginning of time. Genesis 1:27 confirms, "God created mankind in his own image, in the image of God he created them; male and female he created them."

Watching your daughter—being a student of who she is and what makes her tick—will give you advantages when it comes to understanding all the women who pass through your life. That includes your wife, coworkers, bosses, neighbors, friends, your daughter, and her friends.

Insight for GirlDads: Sons vs. Daughters

With my sons, I was more of a sparring partner. They had me walking through life with a rough-and-tumble attitude, and I'm not sure I spent much time thinking deep thoughts or feeling deep feelings. With boys, actions take precedence over feelings. When your son picks up a pinecone, he chucks it at a stump. With boys, you tend to explore the world shoulder to shoulder. Together, you might imagine what's over the next hill—or even over the horizon—but the adventure is in the journey, and you don't often stop to smell the roses.

Watching my boys grow, I was very much aware of benchmarks along the way. Their first soccer game. Their first sleepover. When I could throw a baseball as hard as I could and they were able to catch it without flinching. The landmark moments when I introduced them to power tools, deodorant, the fuse box, the lawn mower, and how to shake hands, change a tire, tie a tie, or set a mousetrap.

I was far from perfect, but I have a sense that my sons, Alec, Randall, Max, and Isaac, saw me as a model or yardstick to measure themselves against. Certainly, they didn't have to follow in my career footsteps, but they knew they were expected to finish school, get a good job, go to church, and find a good woman to marry.

Daughters bring out an entirely different side of their dads. It's not going through life shoulder-to-shoulder and growing a list of accomplishments. With girls, it's about doing life face-to-face (or even nose-to-nose) and growing your own capacity for tenderness, intimacy, and empathy.

Said another way, when your daughter finds a pinecone, it becomes not a projectile to be thrown, but a treasured keepsake reminding her of that walk in the woods with daddy.

Insight for GirlDads: The New and Improved You

I hope you can see that the world could use a few more men with the traits naturally acquired in your role as a girl dad. Because you have committed to being in tune with your daughter, you will very likely pause a little more often to consider the world around you. You'll appreciate the here and now. You may find yourself becoming a bit more supportive, cooperative, affectionate, and nurturing. Does that scare you? It shouldn't.

Please don't worry that this new and improved version of yourself will undermine your masculinity. As an adult male, you are still very much expected to spit, whittle, flex in the mirror, scream at umpires, blow your nose in the shower, go ice fishing, go axe throwing, and hog the remote. Those activities will not endear you to your daughter (or your wife), but that's not what we're talking about here.

Think of it this way. Because you want to spend more time with your daughter, this is your chance to sincerely look for ways to make yourself more agreeable, lovable, helpful, and user-friendly. It's not magic. It's logical. Even practical.

Dad, you may think, *That's not my style.* You may even profess that you're stuck in your ways. But you don't have to be.

Hey, you've made it all the way to the last chapter of this book, so I'm pretty sure you have the wherewithal to do a little self-analysis. Consider areas in your life that may benefit from a little tweaking. Surely somewhere in these pages you've seen a glimpse of yourself and thought you might want to up your game. Think hard. If you dare, ask your daughter. If you double dare, ask your daughter's mother.

Insight for GirlDads: God Bless the Differences

When I consider Rae Anne—and when you consider your own daughter—let's admit that there are a few things about them that drive us crazy.

With Rae, it's a short list, and I won't be going into detail. But daughters and dads will always have differences. After all, we're looking at the realities of life from different perspectives. We're different genders, born decades apart into vastly different worlds, and have different gifts and experiences. If we accept that fact, I believe those differences can actually bring a vibrancy to our relationship.

Consider the amazing diversity God has woven into all of creation and how that makes our lives so much richer. If our kids were our clones, what fun would that be?

Even though you and your daughter are quite different, the goal is to share a sense of honor and integrity that goes beyond human understanding. When you're in the same room, you should be able to look at each other and trust that both of you have each other's best interests in mind. Even if you're in disagreement about a minor issue, the mutual conviction is that love, respect, honesty, and faith will prevail.

I am confident that at the end of the day and the end of our lives, Rae Anne and I will always know that we're there for each other. I pray that same secure feeling for you and your daughter.

Rae Anne's Reality Check

While living vicariously through your children is not something I will ever advise a parent to do, what I do encourage you to do is embrace the new perspective that having a child, particularly a daughter, will give you.

Now, I am not a parent. I do not claim to understand what it means to have a child. What I do know is what it was like for ten-year-old Rae Anne (the youngest child in her family) to hold her first newborn foster brother in her arms for the first time. I recall feeling a natural protective instinct, anger at the kind of world that would take this baby's home and health from him, and marveling at the way his chest would rise up and down. I know what it was like when my nieces and nephews entered my life. Christmas was full of magic again, the future was full of potential, and my love was inexplicably infinite. I know what it is like to watch my brothers bring their children home and to see these men I have known my entire life change before my eyes.

Having a child, having a daughter, changes you. So my advice is to let it. And then rise to the challenge in front of you—the grand challenge of being the most important man in your little girl's life. The beautiful challenge of helping to shape her world. The vital challenge of equipping her for the life she is destined for.

Be the best version of yourself. Be the adult you needed when you were kid. Be the dad she deserves. Do the work. Do it for her.

About My Dad

While my dad lists above all the ways he and I are different, the truth is we are quite similar. Sometimes that is the best thing about our relationship, and oftentimes it is the hardest thing. But when I look back at my life and the relationship we have, what I see is change. Over the years, we have both grown and transformed into a dozen different versions of ourselves. With that came some harsh doses of reality on both sides. He is not a superhero anymore, and I am not a perfect little girl.

But superheroes and perfect little girls are boring, and they don't exist. Instead, we get to be real people who love each other in the midst of pain, support each other while enduring failure, and challenge each other while in conflict. Which also means we get to be the people who rejoice in each other's successes, thrive in each other's company, and find comfort in each other's friendship.

It looks like I get to have the last word here in our book. And I will gladly take it to give you one last charge, one last promise: Dad, the best is yet to come.

About the Authors

Rae Anne Payleitner is in her late twenties. She was a leader in high school, sharing the highest award given out to a handful of seniors at Honors Night. Ranking sixteenth of 620 students academically while staying remarkably well-rounded, Rae was active in speech, band, choir, student government, mock trial, National Honor Society, Fellowship of Christian Athletes, and the school newspaper. Her leadership skills surfaced as a student athletic trainer, wrestling team statistician, basketball captain, and all-state softball catcher, and she was named female athlete of the year—all of which helped her gain entry to West Point Military Academy. There, she hit a three-run home run in the final game of the Patriot League tournament which earned the Black Knights a trip to the NCAA tournament. Two concussions and a serious knee injury effectively ended her military career. After two years at West Point, she attended the School of Business & Law at University College Dublin in Ireland for four years. Rae Anne is currently a data analyst and operational consultant in the Chicago area.

Jay Payleitner is an affable and honest communicator who spent a decade in major market advertising followed by more than two decades producing national radio programs featuring Josh McDowell, Chuck Colson, TobyMac, and other ministry leaders. He is a popular speaker on parenting, marriage, and doing life right. Jay is the author of more than twenty-five books totaling almost a million sold, including *52 Things Kids Need from a Dad, Don't Take the Bait to Escalate, Hooray for Grandparents,* and *What If God Wrote Your Bucket List?* He's a longtime partner of Iron Sharpens Iron and the National Center for Fathering. Jay and his wife, Rita, live near Chicago, where they raised five kids and loved on ten foster babies. There's much more at jaypayleitner.com.

Notes

Preface

1. Lauren Crawford, "ESPN Anchor Is Moved to Tears While Giving Emotional Kobe Bryant Tribute," Fox Sports Radio, January 28, 2020, https://foxsportsradio.iheart.com/content/2020-01-28-espn-anchor-is-moved-to-tears-while-giving-emotional-kobe-bryant-tribute/.

Chapter One: Your Daughter's Hopes and Dreams

1. National Center for Education Statistics, "Table 303.70. Total Undergraduate Fall Enrollment in Degree-Granting Postsecondary Institutions, by Attendance Status, Sex of Student, and Control and Level of Institution: Selected Years, 1970 through 2028," Digest of Education Statistics, 2018 Tables and Figures, https://nces.ed.gov/programs/digest/d18/tables/dt18_303.70.asp.
2. Niall McCarthy, "Women Are Still Earning More Doctoral Degrees Than Men in the U.S.," *Forbes*, October 5, 2018, https://www.forbes.com/sites/niallmccarthy/2018/10/05/women-are-still-earning-more-doctoral-degrees-than-men-in-the-u-s-infographic/?sh=23de023f45b6.

3. National Women's Law Center, "Title IX Fact Sheet: Debunking the Myths about Title IX and Athletics," August 2015, https://nwlc.org/wp-content/uploads/2015/08/title_ix_debunking_myths_8.11.15.pdf.

4. Center for American Women and Politics, "History of Women in the U.S. Congress," Rutgers University Eagleton Institute of Politics, https://www.cawp.rutgers.edu/history-women-us-congress.

5. Deloitte Global Boardroom Program, "Progress at a Snail's Pace: Women in the Boardroom: A Global Perspective," https://www2.deloitte.com/global/en/pages/risk/cyber-strategic-risk/articles/women-in-the-boardroom-global-perspective.html.

Chapter Two: Your Daughter's Teams and Teammates

1. Adapted from Jay Payleitner, *The Little Book of Big Ideas for Dads and Daughters* (Eugene, Oregon: Harvest House, 2017), 26–7, 138–39.

2. Adapted from Jay Payleitner, *10 Conversations Kids Need to Have with Their Dads* (Eugene, Oregon: Harvest House, 2014), 43–44.

Chapter Three: Your Daughter's Friends

1. Tara Haelle, "Girls Three Times More Likely to Self-Harm Than Boys—and Need Help," *Forbes*, October 19, 2017, https://www.forbes.com/sites/tarahaelle/2017/10/19/girls-three-times-more-likely-to-self-harm-than-boys-and-need-help/?sh=11958df427a0.

Chapter Four: Your Daughter's Mom

1. Adapted from Jay Payleitner, *52 Things Kids Need from a Dad* (Eugene, Oregon: Harvest House, 2010), 167–68.

Chapter Six: Your Daughter's Brokenness

1. Adapted from Jay Payleitner, *52 Things Daughters Need from Their Dads* (Eugene, Oregon: Harvest House, 2013), 111–13.

Chapter Seven: Your Daughter's Boyfriends

1. Adapted from Jay Payleitner, *10 Conversations Kids Need to Have with Their Dads* (Eugene, Oregon: Harvest House, 2014), 135–36.

2. Joe S. McIlhaney Jr., Freda McKissic Bush, and Stan Guthrie, *Girls Uncovered* (Chicago: Northfield Publishing, 2012), 37, 41, 46.

3. Ibid, 54.

4. David Cantor et al., "Report on the AAU Campus Climate Survey on Sexual Assault and Sexual Misconduct," Westat, revised October 20, 2017, https://www.aau.edu/sites/default/files/%40%20Files/Climate%20Survey/AAU_Campus_Climate_Survey_12_14_15.pdf.

Chapter Eight: Your Daughter and Her Self-image

1. Kerri Boutelle et al., "Weight Control Behaviors among Obese, Overweight, and Nonoverweight Adolescents," *Journal of Pediatric Psychology* 27, no. 6 (September 2002), 531–40, https://doi.org/10.1093/jpepsy/27.6.531.
2. South Carolina Department of Mental Health, "Eating Disorder Statistics," 2006, http://www.state.sc.us/dmh/anorexia/statistics.htm.
3. M. E. Collins, "Body Figure and Preferences among Preadolescent Children," *International Journal of Eating Disorders* 10, no. 2 (March 1991): 199–208, https://www.mobap.edu/wp-content/uploads/2013/01/nedsp2007_eating_disorders_fact_sheet.pdf.
4. Jon Arcelus et al., "Mortality Rates in Patients with Anorexia Nervosa and Other Eating Disorders. A Meta-Analysis of 36 Studies," *Archives of General Psychiatry* 68, no. 7 (July 2011): 724–31, https://doi.org/10.1001/archgenpsychiatry.2011.74.

Chapter Nine: Your Daughter and Her Time with You

1. Excerpted from Jay Payleitner, *The Little Book of Big Ideas for Dads and Daughters* (Eugene, Oregon: Harvest House, 2017), 152–54.